It Takes a Lifetime to Become Yourself

BY

KAY CARMICHAEL

Edited by

David Donnison

Scotland Street Press

EDINBURGH

The Author

Kay Carmichael was born in 1925 and died in 2009.
After an impoverished upbringing in Glasgow's East
End, she became a social worker, university teacher,
wife of an MP, a member of the Scottish Office
Advisory Committee for setting up Children's Panels,
a peace activist (for which she was imprisoned), and
an advisor for Harold Wilson's Policy Unit at No.
10 Downing Street. The collection is edited by her
husband, David Donnison.

Published by Scotland Street Press 2017

2 5 7 3 1 2 9 7 5 8

First published in Great Britain in 2017 by
Scotland Street Press
Edinburgh
www.scotlandstreetpress.com

Cover Design by Bookmark Studio
www.bookmark-studio.com

ISBN: 978-1-910895-17-7
Typeset in Scotland by Bookmark Studio

Printed and bound in Scotland by Airdrie Print Services

In a Rearview Mirror

This is not a book; it's more a conversation. My intention is to share some experiences, some ideas, some thoughts.

Some of what I write about is long past, lost in my personal history, but as alive to me as if it happened yesterday rather than nearly eighty years ago. Much of those early happenings is ugly which is perhaps why I remember them so clearly. On the other hand age seems to bring with it a kind of clarity. But I don't want to stay mourning in the past. Rather I hope that I can learn something about survival and learning how to be human. To do that I have to explore what being human means.

A hand-written note found in Kay's papers.

Contents

Foreword

More than forty years ago, Kay Carmichael and I were colleagues on the Supplementary Benefits Commission, now long gone, which had a general responsibility for Britain's means-tested social security benefits. We were still cautiously getting to know each other. Making a working visit together to social security offices in Glasgow, her home town, she invited me to come with her for a brief trip to her tiny cottage in Argyll before I returned to London. Driving her Mini over the spectacular Rest and Be Thankful pass, she began talking about a book she wanted to write. 'Social scientists…', she said, '…are always going on about the life-long handicaps suffered by people who had a hard time in childhood. But there are some people who survive a bad start and do quite well. How do they achieve that? That's the question I want to write about.' We had an interesting conversation about this before returning to the city, but many years passed before I realised it was her own story she was talking about. She was to write three other books, but never this one.

Later we became life partners, and eventually husband and wife. When she died on December 26th, 2009, she left me many of her papers. They described her childhood and youth: there were articles she wrote for the press, notes for speeches she gave, ruminations and reflections of various kinds, and lots of poems. In the years before her death she sifted through these papers and shredded many of them, so I think we can assume she was happy to let other people read those that remain.

This is not a draft of the book she once had in mind. Nor is it an autobiography, although early chapters were inspired by a plan she once had for writing one. It is a selection of her writings about many different subjects, starting with vivid accounts of her childhood and youth. After that there is a long silence through the years when she married Neil Carmichael, gained her higher education in Glasgow and Edinburgh Universities, raised their daughter Sheena, took the first steps in a professional career as a social worker, helped to get Neil into Parliament, and did much of the work of running his constituency – the constituency in which they lived. I asked her from time to time about these years, but she was reluctant to talk about them and I feel she is entitled to her privacy. Some of her writings from later times are presented in the second half of this book, followed by a selection of the poems that she wrote, some of which I have spliced into earlier chapters dealing with the events that inspired them.

She describes the early years of the campaign for nuclear disarmament and the brief imprisonment it brought her; the creation of the Special Unit for violent prisoners in Barlinnie Prison – Scotland's biggest jail – in which she worked part-time; the three months she spent living on a very low income in a council flat in Glasgow's East End; a life-changing week in a Buddhist monastery in Japan, and finally her gallant approach to her own death.

In order to present Kay's writings in a way that is easiest to understand, I have had to select and combine passages written at different times, and occasionally to add brief stories that she told me that were never written down. But this is her book, not mine; a collection of her thoughts and experiences, not a biography. Her writings fill most of the book. They are presented in non-italic font. My own much briefer contributions are printed in italics.

Towards the end of the book I offer a few thoughts about the conclusions Kay might have drawn from her own story for the question she posed forty years earlier on our journey through the mountains of Argyll.

Sooner or later, many of us have to survive the loss of the person who gave meaning to our lives. I tried to find my own way through this catastrophe by writing poems, which, together amount to a requiem for Kay. I offer them as a postscript to this, her book, hoping that they may help others going through these bleakest of years.

I shall be placing Kay's papers in the archives of Glasgow University's library where they can be consulted by readers who want to explore the original documents from which this book is constructed, and who desire to learn more about the life and times of an extraordinary woman.

David Donnison
Glasgow, 2017

Main Events in Kay's Life

Kay never told me she was writing an autobiography, but among her papers I found early drafts of its first chapters. A selection of these appear in the following sections. Like all good autobiography, it is also therapeutic writing – an attempt to reflect on early, and sometimes painful, experiences, and to learn from them. But she abandoned this project and worked instead on articles, lectures, poems, and eventually three books. These writings can be found in Glasgow University's library and its archives. Since she often wove personal experiences into her writings, it will be easier for readers to understand them if they know the main events in her life. I briefly note them in the pages that follow. Some of the dates given are approximate, and the reader will note there are large gaps in the story for years I know nothing about.

November 22nd, 1925 Kay's birth in Glasgow.

1928 Her father left home. Kay and her mother went to live with her grandmother and two of her mother's sisters in a room and kitchen in Shettleston, in Glasgow's East End.

1929 Kay's mother began training as a midwife, and placed four-year-old Kay in a convent boarding school in Girvan, South Ayrshire, where she was brutally treated, but learned to read.

1931 Kay got polio, was placed for six months in the Glasgow Royal Infirmary, and left her school.

1932 Discharged from hospital, Kay returned to her grandmother in Shettleston. For three years wore a metal frame to support her paralysed arm. She did not attend school, but read daily in the Tolcross public library.

1934-35 Her father returned to live with Kay and her mother. He removed the frame from her arm and got her back into school – a Protestant school.

1936 Her father left them, and her parents got divorced. She saw him only briefly thereafter, in the 1960s. Kay and her mother returned to her grandmother in Shettleston, and Kay was transferred to a Catholic school. Her mother, working as a midwife, became increasingly alcoholic.

1939 As war began, Kay persuaded her mother to get her evacuated. She was taken to Dumfriesshire where she lived at first on a chicken farm, and went to the local school.

1940 She was transferred to The Rigg, a pig farm three miles from the school to which she walked each day. She returned from time to time during school holidays to her mother in Glasgow – as briefly as possible.

1941 She was transferred to a new billet in the home of the local Minister, who had a mental breakdown and disappeared in company with his wife.

1941 Kay was transferred to Trigony, the large and beautiful home of Mrs. Dickson, a wealthy widow who treated her as a guest – a transformative experience.

1942-43 She returned, aged seventeen, to live with her mother in Blair Street, Shettleston. She was the 'dux' – the top scholar – in her secondary school. She joined the youth section of the Independent Labour Party (I.L.P.), which she later described as the most important higher education she received, and explored various radical and eccentric groups meeting in Glasgow's East End. She had a spell of treatment from a psychoanalyst at about this time.

1944 She entered Glasgow University as a medical student.

1945 (or thereabouts) Her father left the army, with the rank of colonel, and went to Rhodesia. He wrote to Kay inviting her to join him there but she did not reply.

1946 She was suspended from the University following failure in exams due, she believed, to brain damaging effects of polio – and, perhaps, to lack of early schooling which always made mathematics difficult for her.

It was at about this time that Kay left the I.L.P. to join the Labour Party, feeling it was her duty to transform it into a radical movement ('The first of my political failures', she was later to comment.)

1948 Kay married Neil Carmichael, fellow member of the I.L.P., leaving her mother's home and the Catholic Church.

1949 Their daughter Sheena was born.

1952 They moved to Hyndland in Glasgow's West End – an aspirational step, prompted by Kay and funded by James Carmichael, M.P., – Neil's father – who was the last I.L.P. M.P.

1955-57 Kay entered Glasgow University to take the two-year Certificate in Social Study. She worked as District Secretary for the Glasgow Society of Social Service at about this time. Sheena was placed for a year in Kilquanity House, a progressive private boarding school.

1958-60 Kay took the diploma course in mental health – a training for psychiatric social work – at Edinburgh University. Formed a life-long friendship with her supervisor, Megan Browne.

1959 Kay's mother became ill with cancer, Kay regularly visiting her in hospital. She worked at this time in Dr, Fred Stone's Child Guidance Clinic, in Glasgow; and later (or earlier?) with borstal girls.

1960 Her mother died. Kay invited to join Glasgow University's staff as a tutor in social work and Deputy Director of the training course for probation officers – Scotland's first. Later she took an M.A. by dissertation (on borstal girls), as required for appointment to a lectureship.   She also held a part-time post as a probation officer – her clients visiting her in the University.

1962 Neil won a by-election to Parliament for Glasgow Woodside, the constituency in which they later came to live when its boundaries were changed..

1963 Kay appointed as a lecturer in social work – later transferring to social administration. With Neil now in London for most of the week, she was helping to run the constituency for him, and providing lunches in her home for about a dozen activists on Sundays.

1964 The publication of the report of the Kilbrandon Committee, appointed by the Government to review Scotland's juvenile courts, social work, and child care services, led to the appointment of a small working party to propose extensive changes. This group – consisting of Richard Titmuss, Professor of Social Administration at the London School of Economics; Megan Browne, previously Kay's tutor at the University of Edinburgh, and Kay – gave advice that led to a white paper, 'Social Work and the Community', (cmnd.3065) presented to the Westminster Parliament in 1966. Its recommendations led to the Social Work (Scotland) Act of 1969, creating Scotland's social work service, which brought together various services previously based in separate departments, and to the creation of the Children's Panels which replaced the juvenile courts in Scotland.

This work brought Kay into contact with the academic, administrative and political worlds of London, leading in time to her appointment as a member of the Supplementary Benefits Commission, which had a general responsibility for Britain's means-tested social security benefits; her part-time membership of the Policy Unit set up by Harold Wilson at No. 10 Downing Street; and membership of the B.B.C's Scottish Advisory Committee.

1973 Kay played a part in setting up the Special Unit in Barlinnie prison for prisoners serving life sentences who had proved dangerously unmanageable in other Scottish prisons. For some years after this she worked in the Unit as a social worker for one day a week.

1974 Kay appointed as a senior lecturer in social administration, Glasgow University.

1975 Kay appointed Deputy Chair of the Supplementary Benefits Commission.

1976 She took three months leave from the University and her other duties to live in Lilybank, a poor neighbourhood in Glasgow's East End, living on the income she would have received as a single woman living on supplementary benefit. Four B.B.C. television programmes followed, in which she played a leading role as presenter.

1977 Kay presented 'Thought for the Day' on the B.B.C's Today programme. Christopher Sharpe – her first grandchild was born – followed in 1979 by Victoria her granddaughter.

1979 The 'Faslane Horticulturalists' ('Horts' for short) a group of women peace activists, was formed. (Among other demonstrations, the group – which is still active – planted bulbs and potatoes in nuclear bases to reclaim the land for the people.) Kay was an active member till the end of her life.

1980 The Supplementary Benefits Commission was abolished and Kay returned to full-time work in Glasgow University.

1981 Kay retired from the University and joined Strathclyde Region's Social Work Department where she was in charge of services for offenders. She joined forces with David Donnison, previously chairman of the S.B.C, and by now professor of town and regional planning at Glasgow University. They lived in Holyrood Crescent.

1982 Kay started a regular column entitled 'Saints & Sinners' for New Society magazine, for which she had written from time to time. This column continued till 1985, amounting in total to about 200 articles. She was also writing and broadcasting for other media during these years – including a weekly discussion of books, drama, and films for the B.B.C Radio Scotland arts programme – and joined the National Union of Journalists.

1984 Kay accompanied David who worked for a term in the University of Hong Kong. On their way home they went to Burma for two weeks, where David was born and spent his early years. There they travelled widely as guests of Burmese friends of David's parents.

1986 Kay imprisoned in Cornton Vale Prison for refusing to pay a fine imposed for breaking into the nuclear submarine base at Faslane in the course of a Horts' demonstration. She was released after four days when Helen Liddle M.P., prompted by Joe Haines (press secretary to Harold Wilson and Jim Callaghan) and other London friends paid her fine.

1987 She and David moved to Ardentinny, on the shores of Loch Long. They got married – holding parties to celebrate the occasion in Ardentinny, Glasgow, and London.

1988 Visiting Japan with David, Kay spent a week in a small Naikan Buddhist monastery – a life-changing experience.

1988 Death of Harry McShane,.another of her left-wing heroes with whom she had kept in close touch.

1991 Her first book, published by Macmillan, 'Ceremony of Innocence – Tears, Power and protest', dealing with the physiology and psychology of tears, their cultural and political significance – arguing that our ability to express feelings is fundamental to human social development and our capacity to challenge injustices.

1993 'For Crying Out Loud!', a shorter, popular version of her previous book – is published by Argyll. ('An inspiring book. Required reading for anyone who has ever felt ashamed of crying' commented Emma Thompson.)

1993 death of Megan Browne, her tutor on the Mental Health course at Edinburgh University and a life-long friend.

1994 Kay moved with David from Ardentinny to Bank Street in Glasgow where she lived for the rest of her life. It was in this year that Barlinnie Prison's Special Unit, in which Kay had for years worked part-time, was closed. It was also the year when Tony Blair became leader of the Labour Party, which prompted her to leave the Party. She joined the Scottish Socialist Party soon afterwards, leaving it some years later when it imploded, and joining the Scottish National Party, in which she remained for the rest of her life.

2000 Kay completed her Ph.D, for which she had worked in Glasgow University's Centre for Theology, Literature and the Arts.

2001 Death of Neil Carmichael, Kay's first husband. She visited him regularly in the Clydebank care home where he spent his last months.

2003 Kay's book 'Sin and Forgiveness. New responses in a changing world' published by Ashgate; a revised version of her doctoral thesis in which she drew on literature and art to formulate a post-Christian morality. ('In this compulsively readable and passionately argued book [she] has helped us to forge a new ethic for a confused world' commented Richard Holloway.)

December 26th, 2009 Kay's death, at home in Bank Street.

It Takes a Lifetime to Become
Yourself

I

CHILDHOOD

I graduated in failure at an early age. To be precise it was at the moment I slid, gummy and bloody, out of my mother's body and it was seen that I lacked the little pipe in my groin that would have made me a success. When the midwife said 'It's a girl', my parents' faith faltered and their marriage was doomed. It was my fault for being what I am. With my birth they lost faith in each other and in the possibility that they could create the world they sought. I don't know if that little pipe would have persuaded my father to try harder to forgive me and my mother, but she was convinced that for his own reasons he had needed me to be a son, perhaps to placate his own Highland-born mother who was proud of having produced five of them. My mother was also in trouble as it became clear that my too enthusiastic birth had torn her apart so fiercely that access to that part of her body no longer gave her pleasure, only pain. This was clearly my fault.

I learnt about this in great detail. My mother had no one else to talk to, and in the years to come I became the unwilling recipient of intimate details, ranging from knowledge that I didn't understand to knowledge that I would have preferred not to understand. The marriage hung together until I was three years of age, too young to make any sense of the shouting and arguments that dominated their lives. Unable to talk about the true passionate needs and desires that were driving them apart, they expressed these through the absurdity of their differing religious beliefs.

Glasgow, where we lived together so uneasily during these three years, was a hotbed of religious conflict between Roman Catholics and Protestants, with a good dash of anti-Semitism thrown in. My mother was a Roman Catholic. Not, I think, a particularly observant one since, in order to appease my father's mother, her marriage and my baptism had taken place in the splendid Glasgow Barony Church, a bastion of Protestant rectitude. However, under stress, she reclaimed her faith, verbally at least. My Protestant father was conventionally arrogant about Roman Catholic superstitious beliefs and social inferiority. Only her beauty, set off by her stunning auburn hair and dramatic temperament, could have persuaded him to defy his draconian mother and marry a Catholic. Trapped in this marriage he was now finding intolerable, with a daughter rather than the son he had hoped for and a literally unapproachable wife, he reverted to primitive prejudices.

I must have picked up, as I believe children do from birth onwards, the tensions banging from wall to wall in that small flat. My own contribution of the demands that infants make, crying and demanding attention, did not help. Nor did my father's commitment to the Territorial Army; a splendid excuse to get away and be a man among other men. One of the many stories my mother told me later was of her belief that when he went away on these week-end trips with the army he was seeing other women. She was fiercely jealous of him, and I imagine their encounters when he returned from these times away must have exercised her dramatic temperament to its utmost. That which had charmed him as a bachelor no longer had any appeal for him as a husband.

I do not know who left whom. I think it was she who broke first, expecting some response from him. But he did not pursue her or make any attempt to persuade her to return to him. Equally he expressed no wish to see his daughter again. I think I may have wanted to see him. I missed his smell, his bulk (he was a big, tall man), his voice and the roughness of his skin.

Living with my grandmother

My mother had no option but to return to her mother's home, and this gave me my grandmother – the one great gift from my family for which I shall always be grateful. It was with her that I came into consciousness and learned the possibility of being unreservedly loved. She saved my sanity.

My grandmother was a peasant-like woman who took me onto her capacious lap when I needed comfort. The reason for needing it didn't matter – she was always there for me. As a child in Ireland, during one of their famines, she had been put on a boat by a religious organisation attempting to respond to a national tragedy of poverty and hunger. She ended up in a convent in Liverpool with only a ticket around her neck with her name on it – Catherine Brannan – to give her an identity. She had no idea where she had come from. The nuns trained her as a servant and eventually sent her out to work for a middle class family whose son soon made her pregnant. She was promptly sacked.

Then her luck changed. She married a handsome, moustached glass blower working for Pilkington's. They had three girls and were then transferred to Glasgow where the firm was setting up another factory. He joined the army at the beginning of the First World War, survived till near its end, and was then gassed.

Returning home in 1918, he died three weeks later. His large framed photograph, in army uniform, dominated the small room of the 'room and kitchen' where my mother and I now joined my grandmother and two more of her daughters.

It would have been better for my grandmother if her husband had been killed before the war ended. The War Office deemed that his death could not be attributed to enemy action so she was given no pension. She was therefore condemned to live on the Parish until her daughters were old enough to go to work and support her. The Parish money was not posted to her. She had to walk to a hall in Parkhead and queue to collect a mixture of money and contempt. She would often take me with her, leading me by the hand. It was my first experience of sensing a grown-up person's fear – and her relief as she walked away with the few shillings in her hand.

The room and kitchen in which we lived was on the ground floor of a two-story tenement standing on the main street of what had originally been the village of Shettleston in Glasgow's East End. *Kay took me to see it, standing dusty and deserted shortly before it was demolished in one of Glasgow's last slum clearance schemes. The big London Road police station, close to Celtic's Parkhead football ground, now stands on the site.*

I was now living in a Roman Catholic family and on the instruction of our visiting priest was taken for a second baptism. This, he said, would save my soul and eliminate all traces of my previous, corrupt, Protestant baptism. The role of these local priests, who visited all Catholic homes regularly, was to identify any sign of lapsed Catholicism, check that everyone in the family was going to Mass and Confession, sit at the kitchen table, drink a cup of tea, have a biscuit, and expect a donation to Church funds before they left. They behaved like policemen of the soul, and worried parents would ask them to come in and talk to an unruly daughter or sullen son.

The tenement retained many of the characteristics of a village community. Everyone knew everyone else's business. They could be savagely critical, as some were of my mother's failed marriage, but they could also be totally relied on for help when it was needed.

There were three flats on each landing of the tenement. The middle one was a 'single end' consisting of one room in which the family slept and lived. Those on each side – the 'rooms and kitchens' – had two rooms. On each landing was a lavatory used by all three flats on that floor. Every family had their own pieces of cut up newspapers for wiping themselves.

On the top landing lived the terrifying Mrs. Brown, who made it her business to know and comment on everyone else's behaviour. A devout Calvinistic Protestant, she set standards for everyone – most of them admirable but not all attainable. Attending church every Sunday, she brought back the atmosphere of the pulpit, supervising the regularity with which the stairs were swept, washed and their edges marked out with chalk, and the lavatories cleaned and scrubbed. She had all the qualities of a good hospital matron of the old-fashioned sort – a terrifying but also a comforting figure of the kind I would be introduced to in a few years time.

For some reason, my grandmother's habit of going to The Drum, our local pub, on a Saturday night to drink a pint of beer in the best English tradition was exempt from Mrs. Brown's criticism. Her condemnation of our family was reserved for what she saw as my mother's scandalous behaviour in losing a husband.

My grandmother lived in the front close with a newsagent as her neighbour. Our lavatory was set in the back close that led out to the back court. I remember it as a large, comfortable space of bare, scrubbed wood, which held you comfortably above the pan, with a chain comfortably within my reach. The back court was a bare area of ground where there was a midden for rubbish and a shared wash house. It was also used as a playground by children.

The wash house played an important part in the lives of the tenants. Having only a cold water tap in their rooms, the washing of bed linen and larger articles of clothing was done there on a strict rota basis, also supervised by Mrs. Brown. It was an elaborate ritual. A fire was lit under the boiler, which had first to be filled with water through a rubber pipe from a cold tap. The clothes were boiled, then transferred with a long stick to one of two large tubs to be rinsed in cold water. A large mangle, set between two sinks, was used to wring them before they were hung out on ropes, to which they were fastened with clothes pegs and supported by clothes poles to dry in the back court. If it was a rainy day the clothes had to be hung out on the pulleys, which were suspended from the ceilings of everybody's kitchen, including the one-room single ends.

My mother and I slept in the room of my grandmother's room and kitchen. She had brought some furniture with her, so we had a luxuriously covered sofa in a silky black and red pattern – totally inappropriate in that tiny space – one matching armchair and an upright piano, which she played with inaccurate enthusiasm. There was an open fire, only lit in bitterly cold weather, and a hole-in-the-wall single bed in which my mother and I slept that was curtained over during the day. The windows looked on to the street. At some point my mother disappeared from my life and I moved into my grandmother's bed, a three-quarter size hole in the wall in the kitchen, where I cuddled into her while her two other daughters, my two aunts, lay with their heads on pillows at the opposite end of the bed and their feet around us.

The small house was a model in its use of space. The front door led into a small lobby where coats and shoes were kept. To the right was the room I have already described; to the left, the kitchen. On your left as you entered the kitchen was the coal bunker – the coal needed to keep the fire burning on the opposite wall. This fire heated the oven and was used for boiling water and cooking. Above the fireplace was a gas mantle, which lit the room. To the right was the hole-in-the-wall bed, also with curtains although these were never drawn. Under the windows on the left, looking out on to the back court, was the sink with its swan neck tap, which poured out cold water. There was a small table in the middle of the room with a hinged leaf, which made it possible for everyone to squeeze around it, and on the wall with the coal bunker was a high shelf where precious dishes were stored. Every other inch, including the space under the beds, was used for the storage of clothes, bed linen, towels, tablecloths – and everything else a family could need.

Our family was small compared with some others. On the corner of the building, in a single end on the ground floor, was the family of McElhoneys, consisting of two parents and seven children. They were the despair of Mrs. Brown. To her they represented the worst features of Roman Catholics and particularly Roman Catholics of Irish origin. In the nineteenth century Irish Roman Catholics had flooded into Glasgow and many other cities to escape poverty and hunger. Many had done well, but some, like the McElhoneys, had failed to cope with the transition from a peasant life to the world of the big city. This family, not even in the eyes of the church particularly good Catholics, had held on to their myths and symbols. Their father had painted on the wall above their bed a larger-than-life image of Jesus Christ with his chest slit open to show his bleeding heart. It is a well known icon, but only later in life was I able to appreciate that it may have been Mr. McElhoney's heart that was bleeding.

When my mother disappeared I learned that she had gone to a Catholic maternity hospital on the other side of the city to train as a midwife – although this did not mean anything to me. She had always had aspirations to better herself. Having left school at the age of eleven and got her first job in a fish and chip shop peeling potatoes – work she hated. She graduated in time to become a waitress in 'F and Fs', one of the top Glasgow restaurants. It was here she learnt some of the refinements of the rich and met my equally upward aspiring, lower middle class father who was a junior manager in the Post Office. Over the years she had collected some beautiful things – mirrors, pieces of glass, small painted tables – but her pride and joy was the piano she had taught herself to play.

Her prime fantasy, one of several, was that she was the daughter not of her legal parents but of her mother and some unknown rich and cultivated man. The slender thread on which this hung was the unspoken belief in the family that the eldest of my grandmother's four daughters had been born before her marriage. The fact that this girl left Glasgow as soon as she could, returned to Liverpool, and cut herself off from the rest of us gives the story some credence. Many families have this kind of submerged history. My mother had been born in 1901, although she always pretended it was 1904, which enabled her to claim she was three years younger than her real age. She was deeply jealous of her older sister's uncertain status and clung to the possibility that she herself was in some way socially superior to the rest of the family. She was certainly different.

Living with my grandmother I recall even now as a healing experience. She had a soft, warm and spacious body, which was always available to me – during the night as well as during the day. All our living activities took place in the little kitchen – eating, sleeping, washing, ironing – everything you can imagine other than emptying bladder and bowels – which took place in the lavatory outside in the close – and clothes washing, which took place in the outside wash house in the back court. I slept with my grandmother and my two aunts in the small set-in bed in the kitchen. When my mother came home for an occasional week-end from her training as a midwife she took me to sleep with her in the even smaller set-in bed in the other room of the house – the room my grandmother had given her to keep the furniture she had retained from her marriage. I was not enthusiastic about that.

I loved sleeping with my grandmother. I felt safe. I couried in to her back and felt her nightdress against my skin. I knew it was white – although I could not see it in the dark – because both of her nightdresses were white. Her back was broad and warm and I felt warm beside her. Before coming to bed she plaited her hair. The plait hung over her shoulder and I could feel it if I moved my head. The bed was soft, and because she made a hollow in it I rolled in to her. She would fall asleep and begin to snore gently. It was a lovely comforting sound. I loved her very much, and even though she was turned away from me I knew she loved me. She was the only person in the world who made me feel safe. Lying in the warmth with the kitchen fire still flickering in the range was the nearest thing I knew to what heaven must be like. As my eyes began to close I felt myself falling asleep. I would waken in the morning to feel her climbing out of bed and would hear her pull out the chamber pot – the po – from under it. I heard the long stream of urine hit the china but I wouldn't move until she had put it away. Then I would turn around and watch her go to the sink and wash.

My mother's social aspirations transferred themselves to me, making her determined that I should be educated. She insisted on my grandmother sending me to the local Catholic school as soon as I reached the age of four. This was a small primary school about a mile up the main road from our house. I was taken and left there without, to my recollection, any explanation of what was going on.

I was introduced at once to the mysteries of the Catechism:

Q. Who made you?

A. God made me.

Q. Why did God make you?

A. God made me to know him and love him in this world and to be happy with him in the next.

Had I known it, all the answers to my questions were being offered for the rest of my life. But I was too terrified by this strange place to understand any of this. Halfway through the morning my need to relieve my bowel overtook my capacity to control it. I was too frightened to ask where I could go to find relief. The result was that, with a loaded pair of knickers, I stumbled out of the school and made my way with tears pouring down my face down the long Shettleston Road to find my grandmother. On my appearing at the door, without asking any questions, she took me in her arms, carried me to the sink, peeled off my knickers, stood me in a basin of the warm water always standing on the stove, and simultaneously washed and comforted me. She refused all appeals by my mother to send me back to school.

Banished to a convent school

But my mother was not to be defeated. A few months later, I was taken away from my grandmother's loving care. I think that was prompted by the fact that I was beginning to call her 'Mam', and my mother found me helping her to scrub the kitchen floor. My next memory, still vivid, is of sitting by myself in a large room with chairs round the wall. A nun came to tell my mother that 'Reverend Mother will see you now' and she was taken away, departing without any explanation. I was not to see her again for several months. For all I knew I would never see her or my grandmother again.

After what seemed a long time, I was collected from this room by a woman in a long black dress, wearing a black veil and having a white cloth around her face. I was not as terrified as I ought to have been. I knew already that what was happening was my fault for being who I was. I switched off feeling. In fact I had been left in a convent run by nuns of the order of Saint Joseph of Cluny in the small town of Girvan, more than sixty miles from Glasgow in South Ayrshire. My mother must have persuaded them to take me as an act of charity. There was no way she could have afforded the fees while she was training as a midwife. That was the beginning of my serious indoctrination into the Roman Catholic faith. It had little or no relationship to the gentle beliefs of my maternal grandmother.

I came to understand that this place was a convent. The order, they told us with pride, was formed in 1650 and the nuns who ran it dressed in the way they were taught then, and behaved as if nothing had changed since. They wore a black habit and veil with a band of white linen around their foreheads. Swinging in front of them they each wore a large crucifix. My main torturer, as I shall explain, was called Mother Stanislaus. I came to hate her with the pure passion only a child can summon up. In these years there is no place for understanding or modification of feeling. My hatred was a flame that burned with its own beauty, but at the same time I knew that it was sinful. It is not just wrong; it is wicked – sinful. By sending me away from my beloved grandmother – the only person I was able to trust – my heart had been broken. But not my spirit; hatred kept that alive. I learn to fight the nuns in every way I knew how, ranging from wet beds to the rejection of food. They fought back with leather straps, urine-sodden sheets draped round my shoulders, and decomposing plates of food I had refused to eat. The nuns were not – well, most of them were not – consciously cruel to me. They were simply emotionally absent, not only to me, but to all the children. They may have been taken up with their religious practice. It was their devotion to Jesus and a variety of saints that absorbed their emotional lives and there was nothing left over for human beings.

I think the emotional absence of the nuns suited me very well. The brief opportunity I'd had to experiment with trusting my grandmother before losing her would have made it difficult for me to trust anyone else. But that capacity was not asked of me. All that was required was that I be obedient and learn the behaviour, beliefs and rules of this organisation. I managed the behaviour since it merely involved learning to do what you were told. The beliefs tended to pass over my head. I was, after all, not yet five years of age, and although I learned to recite the mantras of the Our Father, the Hail Mary and the great sounding Credo – '...I believe in God the Father Almighty, Creator of Heaven and Earth...' – it would be some years before I saw them as being relevant to my life.

The one exception among the nuns was an aged and crumpled little woman called Mother Theresa, who had returned to Scotland after long years of missionary work in Africa. She taught me to read. I will always be grateful to her for that great gift. I absorbed the letters of the alphabet and the turning of the letters into words as if it was a special kind of air I was breathing. She knew what she was giving me, and somewhere our souls met. It was to be my only good experience in the convent; but for the rest of my life it was the most important. She had given me the gift – the shiver of excitement – I was always to feel on finding a new book. I wanted to read.

The routines of our daily lives were simple. Eighteen of us slept in a dormitory laid out in three rows of six beds. By lifting my head I could see out of the windows to a huge rock in the sea, which I later learned was called the Ailsa Craig. This dormitory and all our daily activities were the responsibility of a Gauleiter type of nun called Mother Stanislaus. She ruled by terror. And was proud of it. I knew, as children do, that she disliked me but not why. Now, with more understanding, I think I was her necessary scapegoat. When she was showing visitors round the school she would send for me and tell them that I was the littlest girl in the school. Then she would say, 'Watch this', hold her finger in front of my face and I would burst into tears. I hated her for being able to do this to me.

A child's hatred is very powerful and can feel wonderful because it overwhelms the pain of loss, of having been abandoned, of having no one. It gives focus and meaning to one's life. The capacity to hate is very important. Its partner is love and its derivation is love lost or damaged. I, like all children, needed love, needed comfort, needed the warm feeling of being valued. I had been given those experiences by my grandmother, but Mother Stanislaus had created for me a world, cold and hostile, in which there was no place for kindness and in which the only plant that could grow and flourish was hate. It was the pure passion only a child can summon up: my hatred for her matching her hatred for me. In these years there is no place for understanding or modification of feeling. The hatred is a flame that burns with its own beauty while at the same time one knows that it is sinful. Hate and love are inextricably enmeshed, and guilt slides away when the self is drowned in hate.

The hatred kept my spirit, my sense of self, alive. I fought Mother Stanislaus in every way I could, ranging from wet beds to the rejection of food. She fought back with punishments, threats, wet sheets draped round my shoulders as I walk to

and sit through breakfast and decomposing plates of food. For months the wet beds defined my relationship with her. She seems to think I do it deliberately to torment her. She screams at me, telling me that I am dirty still to be wetting the bed at five years of age and that it's a sin to cause so much trouble that my bed has to be stripped every morning and my nightdress changed. It's not that I don't try. I try not to go to sleep at night. In the middle of one night I woke and, terrified, wandered down through the dark dormitory to the lavatory in the corner only to find when I got back to my bed that it was wet. *Sixty years later, Kay wrote a poem.*

INCONTINENCE

I still feel it,
the wetness on my neck.
Damp linen
round my legs and feet
tripping me
as I go
prodded down the stairs,
along the corridor
to the refectory.
Wrapped in the sheet
I smell the urine,
I smell myself –
ugly, dirty, as I'm forced
to swallow my porridge.
Forced with it
to swallow my hate.

What I remember most about that time was the feeling of
helplessness. There was nothing I could do to change the trap I was
in. There was no one to help me. I knew the other girls were sorry
for me, but they didn't dare say anything. When Mother Stanislaus
berated me she spoke to the whole dormitory, the three rows of
six beds. One of the Irish girls would smile at me in what I felt was
sympathy, but during the day none of the girls mentioned what
was happening to me. It was a taboo subject. I was different from
them in many ways. They came from well doing Irish families.
Unlike them I had no father, no brothers or big sisters also in the

school. Some of them had aunts who were nuns and they were all
confident Catholics, and, unlike me, with no bad Protestant blood
in them.

From the moment of wakening until bedtime every minute
was planned on the basis that the Devil makes work for idle
hands. The day began and ended with prayer, always impressively
formal because many of the words were unfamiliar and therefore
mysterious. But there was no ambiguity about the bedtime prayers.
Lying in bed, we recited the mantras of the Our Father, the Hail
Mary and the great Credo: 'I believe in God, the Father Almighty,
Creator of Heaven and Earth', etcetera...It would be some years
before I felt all this was relevant to my life.

*For a young child whose experience of mothers and fathers had not
been reliably loving, the meaning of such words must always have been
uncertain.*

Every night we children were taught to prepare ourselves for
death. This was not yet a concept I was familiar with, but I was
soon to learn about it in considerable detail. Death, I was given to
understand, was a gateway to Heaven or to Hell. Our behaviour,
good or bad, would be counted every minute of every day and if
we died in the night and our bad behaviour weighed more than
the good we would go to Hell. I had also to learn what was meant
by the word Hell. The teaching of this was obviously a source
of great pleasure for Mother Stanislaus, who had the care of our
souls. They always told me that I must go to sleep with my arms
crossed over my chest. Then, if I died in the night without sin,
I would go straight to Heaven, which was somewhere up in the
skies. There we would be happy for ever in the company of Jesus,
his mother Mary, all the saints and bevies of angels. God was not
mentioned.

THE LAVATORIAL SURRENDER OF A FIVE YEAR OLD

There was nowhere else
to be alone.
In the dormitory
beds lined the walls.
In the schoolroom
desks crowded the floor.
In the refectory
long tables stretched.
I learned the peace
of a closed door.
The safety of solitude,
the comfort of silence.
In that silence
my thoughts were freed.
The tiles were cool
against my face
and death beckoned me
so sweetly. They had
not yet taught me
that hell was there too.
22.1.96

Obedience was something else. No matter how hard I tried to conform, every night I committed the heinous act of wetting the bed. I can't remember how long my body maintained its protest, but ultimately it gave up. I was not thanked for having at last achieved what I had been told to do. What she did not know and what I did not know was that as a result of this episode some iron had entered into my soul.

I must have been a difficult child. This expressed itself most sharply over food. One morning I was given the usual plate of porridge but on this occasion it had lumps in it. When I took a lump in my mouth I wanted to be sick so I dropped it back into the plate and just sat looking at it. Mother Stanislaus, who supervised our meals as well as our dormitory life, came over and told me to eat it up. I explained about the lumps and was given a lecture about children who were starving because they had no food. I simply continued to look at my plate. Ultimately, in despair at my intransigence, she told me I would get nothing to eat until I cleaned this plate. She didn't realise that this threat held no terrors for me. I wanted to die. The porridge was put before me at every following meal. It was only removed when it was turning green. There were no fridges in those days. On the third day she caved in and I was at last given something I could eat. For the first time I tasted power and repeated it by vomiting back the cod liver oil my mother had said I should have every day. I think I was vomiting her up as well. I had won, and what's more had learned that winning was possible. We had a number of minor encounters after that in which I honed my skills of resistance, learning particularly how to retreat within myself to a place where no one could reach me.

One day my mother came to see me. I wasn't told who had come – I was just sent into the parlour, the same parlour in which she had left me. At first I didn't know who she was, and when I remembered I didn't know what to say. In my head now the images have frozen, accompanied only by a sense of deep sorrow which wrapped itself round me, always still there to touch if I chose.

From the dormitory window I could see the Ailsa Craig, and I learned to use the knowledge that it was one thousand one hundred and fourteen feet high as a mantra to ward off my passionate wish for death to rescue me. The other mantra, embedded in the Hail Mary of the Rosary, 'Now and at the hour of our death', with its background awareness of sin and damnation, was too threatening to use. In the lavatory, the only place I had privacy, I would press my forehead against the wall and want, not to die but not to exist, not to feel the horror of being myself.

Sin

My first formal encounter with the theology of sin came at the age of five when I was being prepared for my First Holy Communion. That was the age when we were expected to understand the nature of the privilege we were to be offered. It was beyond description. We were being allowed to take into our mouths the Body and Blood of Christ, who was the Son of God and who had DIED for our sins. (Forgive the capitals but this is the only way I can attempt to convey the solemnity of these communications.) But in order to receive this Great Gift we had to be shriven of our Sins by confessing them to the priest who would then give us Absolution.

This meant that the dark stains of sin which covered our souls (I saw this as something cloudy and mysterious deep inside me) would be washed away, leaving our souls as white as snow. What was also made clear was that any repetition of sin would bring back the stain and unless one went regularly to confession one's soul would get blacker and blacker. If you were to die in this State of Sin you would go straight to Hell where the Devil lived – another important theological concept I will come to soon.

To reinforce their authority, the adults in this convent constantly threatened us with Hell. When I was first introduced to the fear of Hell I had no idea that I was also being introduced to a set of ideas that stretched back for thousands of years. This four-and-a-half-year-old was expected to carry on an awesome tradition, which had helped to regulate human behaviour throughout that time. The whole idea depends on the notion that in some way or another the body and consciousness survive after death and can experience pleasure or pain. A good life brings its reward in Heaven; a bad life brings eternal punishment in Hell.

Hell was where the Devil lived; a place to which he was entitled to take those people who had died with mortal sins on their souls. Here they would live forever in torment, and that torment consisted of being constantly burning in flames. Jesus had talked to his disciples about 'the fire that shall never be quenched'. Once in Hell there was no escape. You would be handed over to the servants of the Devil. These were called demons. They tortured you, and enjoyed doing it. The nuns and visiting priests gave us detailed descriptions of what went on. Fire and vats of boiling oil were predominant in these. In those days open coal or wood fires were the norm, so flames and awareness of the dangers of being burnt were part of our everyday experience. It was therefore easy to translate that into vivid description of gigantic flames in which we would be consumed – not to die, death would be welcome we were told – our fate would be to burn for ever. We were reminded of times when we might have burned a finger and asked to imagine what it would be like if our whole bodies were suffering in this way.

Pincers pulling out fingernails seemed to give the demons particular pleasure, especially if the child in question was a nail biter. I still have the evidence on the index finger of my right hand of how I bit the nail away from the flesh to leave a deep gap in which the nail no longer grew. When, years later, I read of James Joyce's experience in *Portrait of the Artist as a Young Man* I heard again the authentic voice of the retreat priests who came to visit us. When I saw Bosch's great three-part painting, I was immediately at home in his images of the punishments of Hell.

And you went there for eternity. Of all the theological ideas offered to the five-year-old child that I was, the idea of punishments that lasted for 'eternity' was the most terrifying. This, we were taught, meant 'forever'. I was already struggling with notions of time, never knowing how long my incarceration in the convent was to last. We said prayers that ended up 'for ever and ever, amen', so the words were familiar. What it seemed to mean was that the way things were now is the way they would always be, unless they got worse.

The threat of Hell as a consequence of sin was woven in and out of all discussions of behaviour and of belief in Catholicism. My impression as an adult was that there was less emphasis on its torments than I had experienced as a child. (*Kay and I were at a meeting addressed by Richard Holloway when he was still head of the Episcopalian, or Anglican, Church in Scotland. Asked by one of his audience whether they believed in Hell, Richard said 'Anglicans are far too traditional not to believe in Hell; but far too nice to believe that anyone actually goes there.' A characteristically witty version of what was by then a widely held view.*)

In the year 2007, the new Pope, Benedict, reopened the subject with the complaint that Hell, unlike in the past, was now rarely talked about. Pope Benedict is a theological conservative and his pronouncements seem intended to reverse the more relaxed trend that had been noticeable with recent popes and theologians. He has put Hell and the Devil firmly back on the agenda.

In one sermon he warned the congregation, 'Jesus came to tell us everyone is wanted in paradise, and that Hell, about which little gets said today, exists and is eternal for those who shut their hearts to his love'. According to Pope Benedict, the Devil is 'a real, personal and not merely symbolic presence. He is a powerful reality, a baneful superhuman force directed against God's freedom.' But even these strictures are not as dramatic as those offered in earlier days by Milton and later James Joyce. Sartre summed it up for many of us when he said, 'Hell is other people', to which T.S.Eliot's response was, 'Hell is oneself'.

The thought that what I would now call consciousness, though I had no name for it then, could never be lost or abandoned was unbearable. Even death, which Mother Stanislaus had promised us, and which had often sounded attractive compared with life, now offered no solution. I would always be carrying the burden of those sins I didn't understand. I was surrounded by crucifixes and was constantly reminded of the pain and anguish suffered by Christ for my sins. Guilt was nailed into my psyche as surely as his hands and feet were nailed to the cross. The solution offered to me was perfect obedience to the will of God as it was interpreted to me by the nuns. I couldn't take that way out and clung precariously to the notion of autonomy.

Another possibility offered to us, which seemed to modify the prospect of an eternity in Hell, was the notion of Purgatory. This was discussed as a kind of half-way house between life on earth and what was assumed to be our goal, namely an eternity in Heaven. It was a brilliant invention since it offered hope that if you weren't too sinful and died a good death with the help of a priest, you could go to this place and, after a period of waiting, be admitted to Heaven. Part of your punishment was to be able to look up in to Heaven and see God, Jesus and the Blessed Virgin Mary as well as all the saints and to realise that you would not be able to join them until your allotted time was up. That length of time depended on how you had lived your life, being moderately sinful but at least, most of the time, trying to be good.

You could also get help to shorten the time you spent in Purgatory and you could help other people who had died to shorten their time there. The mechanism for that was certain prayers called novena and also acts of piety. A novena – the word means nine – involved saying prayers like the Rosary for nine consecutive days, or else performing an act of religious devotion. I wasn't sure what that meant, but I was accustomed to hearing words that were never explained to me. The main point was that nobody stayed in Purgatory for ever. You just had to wait to get to Heaven. Again, there were some dilemmas tangled into this. You had to have been baptised as a Catholic to gain entry, and babies who died before there was time to baptise them couldn't get into Purgatory and had to go to Hell along with Protestants and all the other non-Catholics. There was another group of just people who died before Christ came into the world and therefore could not be blamed for not responding to his message. They, it was said, are held in the state known as Limbo, which was neither Heaven nor Hell. (The Roman Catholic Church was the last major Christian Church to hold to this belief but it has now been abandoned, without full clarification, however, of the present position.)

You began to realise that to be baptised as a Catholic and to be a Catholic was more important than anything else in the world. Even more important was to be a Catholic nun. The order of St.

Joseph of Cluny who 'cared' for us was also working in the foreign
Missions. In these countries where people knew nothing about
God and Jesus, where they were pagans who worshipped 'false
Gods', the nuns went about saving babies from Hell by baptising
them.

The order had been established in France in 1650 for the
Christian education of children, and their religious dress was
prescribed at the same time, emphasis being laid on the large brass
crucifix worn on the breast 'as a sure defence against the enemy',
namely the Devil. The Devil was a constant companion in our
lives, waiting round every corner to tempt us into sin. Presumably
this was the same for the nuns.

I don't know what took these women who looked after us into
this order of nuns, what motivated them, what their expectations
were, what they were leaving behind, what they were escaping
from. Saint Joseph was known for his interest in helping people
in communities. This was not an enclosed order that engaged its
life in adoration of the Blessed Sacrament. They ran schools in
many countries – India and Barbados were only two examples
– where they could bring both education and Christianity to
the local children. At some stage of their lives, perhaps at the
menopause, they may have wondered why they were looking after
other people's children instead of having some of their own. Their
stern appearance and rigidity of manner may in some cases have
been covering doubts, anger or even heartbreak. Certainly, with
Mother Stanislaus, something had been responsible for the anger
she constantly carried with her. These women are still alive for me
although they must by now be long rotted in death.

As part of the preparation for our First Holy Communion we
had to practise going to the alter rails and opening our mouths,

then putting out our tongues ready to receive the wafer that was the Body and Blood of Christ. We had to learn the rules. If we sinned between going to Confession and going to Mass but still went to take Communion, our tongues would suffer agonising pain when they received the Host. (We now learned that this was the correct word for the Communion wafer.) Also, we were not allowed anything to eat or drink after supper on the Saturday night until after Mass on the Sunday morning. To take even a sip of water would be a mortal sin.

Those of us who had been baptised as Catholics could have our sins regularly forgiven by going to Confession. Confession was a sacrament to which we were entitled because we had been baptised as Catholics. Protestants had no such opportunities for escape. They faced no future other than Hell. This presented me with some problems. I had picked up in the rows between my mother and father and listening to the gossip between my grandmother and my aunts that my father was a Protestant. He was presumably destined for this terrible place along with everyone else who was not baptised a Catholic. I learned also that I had been baptised twice; once as a Protestant and then my soul was saved by being rebaptised as a Catholic...Another puzzle.

Baptism was also a Sacrament. There were seven altogether, but the only ones we were introduced to at this stage were Baptism, Holy Communion and Penance, which meant Punishment. The word Sacrament meant mystery and we were given to understand that all these matters were shrouded in mystery – which for children is, of course, very close to magic. Most of the time I lived in a world of mystery anyway, never knowing the reasons for anything that happened. I didn't know why I was there except that

I must have committed some terrible sin to be taken away from my loving grandmother and left with these terrible people.

We learned that there were Mortal sins and Venial sins, but this was just an academic distinction because we had the impression that all the sins we committed were Mortal. The main one that threatened us was disobedience – although we were so closely supervised that open disobedience was only ever an aspiration, not a real possibility. There was a host of others to guard against from the moment we woke in the morning till last thing at night when, after prayers, we were warned of the sin of putting our hands under the bedclothes instead of crossing them over our chest. *(Was this to prevent the sin of masturbation?)*

We also had to practice a confession. Filing one after another into the confessional box, meeting for the first time the elderly priest whom we had only previously seen saying Mass on the altar, sitting sideways or behind a screen, waiting to hear what we had to say. We had to start by saying, 'Father forgive me for I have sinned'. He was a nice man who spoke gently and tried to help us find sins to tell him. He must have been bored out of his mind by this procession of small girls desperately trying to find something to say that sounded bad enough to need forgiveness. At the end of the pathetic list of not paying attention, allowing your mind to wander and other trivia – never revealing real thoughts or feelings to him about anything – we had to chant the mantra 'Through my fault, through my fault, through my most grievous fault'. In return you were given a penance – normally a number of Hail Marys, beads of the Rosary in which fifty beads were divided into five decades of ten beads each. Five 'Hail Marys' was fairly standard, a decade was for serious offences and a whole Rosary was unimaginable.

The First Holy Communion was fairly traumatic. Dressed in white, we were vestal virgins. I was terrified that I had done something wrong and that my tongue would be set on fire by the communion wafer. The whole idea of swallowing the Body and Blood of Christ was quite terrifying. We were surrounded by images of Christ's body – sometimes on the cross but there were also statues of him clothed, holding His outer garments apart to show his bleeding heart. The index finger of his right hand was pointing to it. We were told that the origin of this gift to us of Holy Communion could be seen in a picture of Christ sitting at a table with his disciples (the name given to his followers) eating bread and drinking wine and saying to them of the bread, 'This is my body, take ye and eat', and of the wine, 'This is my blood, take ye and drink, do this in memory of me'.

I found much of this quite worrying, although later reading in anthropology assured me that these activities lay well within recognised forms of human religious behaviour. The word religion had of course no meaning for us. We were Catholics, we had the true faith and the rest of the world was Protestant and doomed unless they too became Catholics. The most important Catholic was the Pope who was head of the Church, and because he had been chosen by God to be the Pope was able to tell us what God wanted us to do and not to do. Protestants read something called the Bible and had no one to tell them what God wanted. Good Catholics didn't read the Bible. When we grew up we would discover that there was a list of books good Catholics shouldn't read because to do so would weaken their faith and that was a sin.

One of the things I found difficult was that questions were not encouraged. In fact they were actively discouraged, so after a while

I learned to curb my tongue. The idea of faith puzzled me. It still does.

Being introduced to all this medieval theology, we children were both frightened and entranced at being included in this adult view of the world. Every night we knelt beside our beds to say our prayers. When these were finished we were reminded that if we died during the night and hadn't asked forgiveness for every scrap of sin on our souls, then we would go straight to Hell. We were reminded of Hell's main features, told that the worst thing that would happen to us was not the physical agony we would suffer but being separated from God and Jesus for all eternity. This was a remarkably irrelevant thought to offer small children whose reality was that they had already lost the most important loving influences in their lives. We were unlikely to trust alternative images. (One of the children had panic attacks thinking that the parents who seemed already to have abandoned her had gone ahead of her to Hell. She would willingly have joined them there.)

One dictionary defines fear as 'an unpleasant feeling of apprehension or distress caused by the presence or anticipation of danger.' This definition speaks directly to my experience as a child in the Convent of St. Joseph of Cluny. From the moment I entered that austere building I had felt apprehensive, knowing always that something was wrong but not knowing how to make it better.

Mother Stanislaus, with whom I had most contact, was an artist in the use of the most vitriolic language. She made it clear to me with a variety of adjectives that I was the most disgusting of children, beneath contempt and less than human. This pattern began from the start of my stay in the convent. After listening to threats of Hell and its permanence I began to believe that I was living in a kind of Hell without the flames, since I could see no end to it. Later on in my stay I began to think that even the real Hell, which if Mother Stanislaus was correct I was heading for, could not be worse than what I was experiencing here on earth.

I learned over the weeks and months that followed to stand still and expressionless no matter what was said to me. I knew at some level that she gained pleasure from seeing me show my distress. This was the beginning of my training in hiding the scream behind the smile. It was also the beginning of my understanding that the only really safe place in the world was to be by yourself, alone.

I have tried to understand what would make someone behave in the way Mother Stanislaus behaved to me. While she was unkind to the other girls, her behaviour was never as vicious to them as it was to me. They were aware of this and aware that in some way my pain and unhappiness protected them. I was a classical scapegoat, carrying the sins of our small group. My bedwetting was the excuse, the trigger, that justified the use of words like 'dirty', 'filthy' and others that I didn't understand. I think now that what Mother Stanislaus couldn't tolerate was her inability to control me. My urine flowed in the darkness no matter what she said, no matter how she treated me in her attempts to stop me wetting the bed.

(I suspect there were also elements of class and race in their antagonism. This child had been brought from a poor, working class family in the East End of Glasgow to a middle and lower middle class establishment in a small country town, many of whose staff and pupils came from Ireland. They may have reluctantly accepted her as a charitable duty.

Seventy years or more later, Kay wrote a poem that bore the continuing marks of these memories.)

I LIVE ON THE EDGE

I live on the edge
of madness.
Only a membrane
fine as silk
weaves between my self
and inner caves
where pain and terror lurk.
Behind that skin,
sometimes seen by
my unfocussed eye,
a creature lives,
not mine, but bound to me
in old familiar ways, altering
my vision of the world.
Today the membrane ripped
and loosed not only him
to rampage through my head
but others I should have
killed off long ago
had I known how –
had you been there to help.

Polio

Finally it is too much for me, and on that autumn morning in the
sixth year of my life I wake up paralysed. I was there and yet I
wasn't there. This was happening to someone else and I hovered

above that person, above the bed on which she lay. *(Many adults who have been very close to death have reported such out-of-body experiences.)* The strange thing was, I knew what she was feeling – or rather not feeling. I know now that what she was not feeling was strange. She, I, because the two of us were beginning to merge, had begun to wake unable to move, unable to lift a finger or lift a head off the pillow. Yet we didn't scream in panic, didn't try to call for help...this was our fate...this was punishment for my sinfulness...no longer 'we', I, alone was a sinner. I wasn't sure if this was Hell or just another of the awful things that happened to me in this place.

People come and look at me, they talk to each other across me, they don't know what has happened to me and for the first time nobody says to me that it is my fault. But I know better. They had always told me that I must go to sleep with my arms crossed over my chest so that if I died in the night without sin I would go straight to Heaven. I know I am never without sin because every day I am accused of being wicked and sinful by Mother Stanislaus. My paralysis is a justified punishment.

Later, after the local doctor had sent for an ambulance, I found myself in what seemed like another dormitory, but strangely full of adults. It was Glasgow's Royal Infirmary.

The punishment continued there. But gradually my body began to change. First I could lift my head and that meant that I could be propped up into a sitting up position; propped up also in a wheelchair and it was in this condition that I was taken down to the basement of the hospital, into a room with two women in it who told me that they were going to try to make me better. I remember them as being nice women who talked to me and not just about me. Their plan was to put my arms and legs into basins of very hot water and they explained they would then pass through the water currents of electricity. This might be a bit sore at first but it would help if they could keep passing the electricity through until it was too painful for me to bear. At that point, they said, they would stop.

I, of course, tolerated the pain long past the point when it would have been sensible to cry halt. When I began to think again I wondered if it was my sinfulness that had caused me to become ill in this way. This, combined with the teaching that suffering was good for your soul – the soul was a concept I still didn't understand – made me determined to suffer this electrical current for as long as possible. To do so would clearly be an act of virtue and modify my sinfulness. It may have been an act of virtue and it was certainly very sore, but regretfully seemed to have little impact on the paralysis. So my arms and legs are put into the basins, electricity passed through and I have to tell them when the pain is too much to bear – but I will be a brave girl, won't I, and this will be a chance to redeem myself.

Day after day I go on a trolley into a huge room with seats all round in a semi-circle. Here a doctor in a white coat lifts up my arms and legs, lets them fall down again and talks to the people in the seats, also wearing white coats. I don't understand what he is saying. I don't understand anything, but I've given up trying to understand a long time ago. I don't suppose I ever will understand anything any more or trust anyone any more. I am finding a place inside myself where I can't be reached.

My mother came to me, terrifying me with her noisy tears and with the mantra that was to become the hallmark of her feelings about my illness. 'Dear God, what have I done to deserve this?' I had later to find ways of protecting myself against that particular expression of feeling. In the mean time my defenses collapsed in this new environment. People kept coming and looking at me and talking about me in ways I couldn't understand. But who would expect the six-year-old I now was to understand anything? I didn't know what had happened to me and no one tried to tell me.

Over the next six months great improvements took place. I learned to walk, rather precariously at first, regained the use of my right arm, but my left arm stayed stubbornly flaccid. Regaining the use of my right arm brought with it a marvellous reward. I had, at some point soon after, a visit from two nuns from the Convent. They were strangers to me, were formal in their enquiries about my health, and left quickly. But they left behind a great treasure in the form of a thick book. It was called *Myths of Ancient Greece and Rome* and I found I could turn the pages and escape into another world. I'm sure that they didn't realise that their gift was to offer me a totally different view of the afterlife, in fact of theology in general. Here I found a plethora of Gods who in their persons represented every feeling I'd ever had as well as being beautiful, clever and, astonishingly to me, happy. It was to be many years before I could admit even to myself the influence of this discovery, but that time did eventually come. Meanwhile I had a secret reservoir of hope.

While one part of me was still grateful to be in the peace of the hospital where no serious demands were being made on me and I had now relearned some of my self-preservation techniques, another knew that I was gradually getting better. What would that bring? Above all, I didn't want to go back to the Convent. The only person I could say this to was my grandmother. She used to come in and see me and just sit beside the bed for the visiting hour, in what I could see were old-fashioned clothes, not saying anything. She didn't need to, but I think she was frightened of hospitals. I was able to talk to her in ways I couldn't talk to my mother who would come in with a flurry of words, demanding attention from the nurses and overwhelming me. I wasn't able to talk to her and relied on my grandmother to intercede for me. I needn't have worried. I don't think the nuns wanted back a damaged child – another test I had failed. After their one visit they didn't appear again.

After six months I was considered fit to leave hospital. I could now walk with care and use my right arm but not my left. This limb was incarcerated in a massive iron structure, which held it pointing forwards at right angles from my body. I was to wear this monstrosity for the next three years, only having it removed when my father, meeting me again for the first time since I was three years of age, instructed my mother to remove it. His actual words were, 'Take that thing off her. I don't want to be seen with a cripple.'

II

LEARNING TO LIVE WITH POLIO

After six months in the hospital learning to walk again and to live
with the use of only one arm, I was returned to my grandmother's
house. And there began what I was later to recognise as (with
some interruptions) the happiest three years of my life. What
made my life happy was its simplicity. I had escaped from Mother
Stanislaus and the nuns. I could live without constant reminders
of sin and Hell. And bad memories could be eased by cuddling in
to my grandmother in bed at night. Through her, I was gradually
learning to abandon fear and rediscover trust.

I was still in a good Catholic household. My grandmother's
faith was not particularly active, but she always had money
ready for the priest's visit – barely though she could afford it. My
aunts, her two daughters, were Children of Mary. This rather
odd organisation was a pious confraternity dedicated to the
Virgin whom they called Mary Immaculate. Founded in 1830, its
members were entitled to wear a miraculous medal suspended
on a blue ribbon. On certain holy Sundays they would organise a
procession to walk up Shettleston Road to St. Paul's Church where
Benediction would be held. This was one of the services I enjoyed.
It was the most colourful and vibrant, with candles, and the priest
in his most colourful robes. As one of the smallest children I sat

in the front row, close to sleep with eyes flickering open and shut, seeing this rather dull church transformed. It was here that my sense of beauty was formed by what my eyes could see and my ears hear in the marvelous cadences of the Mass and the faltering but passionate music played on the organ.

I enjoyed taking part in the processions organized by the Church. We were shouted at and ridiculed by the local Protestants and particularly the Freemasons. For the first time I learned the pleasure of being anti-authoritarian while surrounded by a group of people, with whom I had something in common, sharing the experience with me. It seems reasonable to assume that this was where the roots of my later public activities in the Peace movement were first developed. Processions protesting for a variety of causes and others protesting against a variety of injustices were to become a natural part of my adult life. Each of these brought with it that childhood sense, not only of taking part in something of significance, but a sense that, somehow, what I was doing gave my life significance.

I finally lost my religious faith at the age of eight. I never really recovered it though I often had to pretend that I had. Faith functioned as a kind of see-saw: on occasion it supported me and sometimes I felt myself sliding off. I have always known that it is important, operating in many areas other than religion. Those who dismiss it as some kind of aberration are making a grave mistake. It is a source both of the most wonderful art ever seen and of the most appalling cruelty ever perpetrated. It has the capacity to change lives for the better, but also to encourage the infliction of misery. It took me many years to confront that last thought. I still may not have finally cleansed it from my soul. However, I didn't know all this in childhood.

Back from the hospital with my grandmother, I knew that something fundamental had changed for me. I was seven now, and had learned to look at the people round me with a certain detachment. It would be absurd to say that I felt betrayed. I knew neither the word nor the concept. All I knew was that the world was now a different shape from that which I had known before going to the convent. My body too was a different shape, my left arm suspended in mid air in a metal frame fastened round my ribs.

I was never told the purpose of this contraption. It was taken off at night, but my only daytime release from its clutches came when, once a week, I had a massage from an Irishman, probably gay, called Michael Cooney. Michael was an authentic Irishman who lived in the top flat in a single end, in the close round the corner from my grandmother in Chester Street, making an uncertain living as a masseur. I have no idea why he had left Ireland, although Glasgow was a common goal for the Irish, or how and why he had become a masseur. All I know is that each week, after I had climbed alone up the three flights of stairs to his door, he gave me a quality of loving care that penetrated even the fearsome defence mechanisms I had erected. He was the first of a number of men who were healers whom I was to meet in my life. He made it possible for me to recognise them. He also, I now realise, taught me without words to accept my paralysed arm; not to reject it, but in a matter-of-fact way to see it as part of myself. He detested my metal cage, would happily have thrown it in the midden, but – as can happen even now – the power of the doctors overwhelmed his intuitive wisdom.

I felt that he was mildly sceptical about the next stage of my journey. I had been told that I was going on a pilgrimage to Lourdes to have my paralysed arm healed. I didn't know where

Lourdes was, I didn't know what a pilgrimage was, I didn't ask and no one explained. As usual I felt detached from the adults who talked around me.

My mother came with me and I think the local parish church must have helped to pay for this exercise in faith because she could not have found the money for herself. For me it was to be an experience of enormous significance.

Pilgrim to Lourdes

I found myself identified as a pilgrim who would receive a miracle and regain the use of my paralysed arm. There was a great deal of talk about miracles around me. I had a sense of something magical – something powerful in which I was to be involved. There were sideways glances at me and my body armour. I stayed detached from the adults who seemed caught up in the excitement of sharing in a profoundly religious experience. I realise now that this was an illusion: the experience had a hysterical edge; people were sharing in magic rather than religion.

We travelled with a group of pilgrims on the S.S. Athenia, a passenger liner built in Glasgow and launched in 1923. The ship was a joy for me, exposing me to experiences that charmed my senses – developing the aesthetic experiences I had been given by the Church services I had attended from the convent school in Girvan. There were large dining rooms, beautifully set tables, smoking rooms with wonderful chairs and sofas, decks where people sat in deck chairs; and I had the freedom to wander through all these places while my mother found people to talk to. She and I shared a small cabin and it was down the corridor outside this cabin that I was to discover the marvellous sensuous joy of a shower. I had never even heard of such a procedure for washing oneself. Coming from my grandmother's room and kitchen, with only a cold tap to supply one's needs, it was a transformative revelation of how it was possible to live. The S.S. Athenia was to achieve the distinction of being the first ship to be sunk in the Second World War. Heading west into the deep Atlantic, she was carrying over one thousand civilians, including three hundred Americans hurrying home to avoid the war.

Lourdes' reputation as a centre of pilgrimage was derived from the belief among Catholics that in 1858 the Virgin Mary appeared to a young girl called Bernadette Soubirous, telling her that many people would come in procession to be healed in waters of the spring flowing from the grotto where she stood. She was taken through the usual procedures of being questioned by the parish priest who was sufficiently convinced to call in his religious superiors to examine her. The Church is cautious about apparitions on both theological and practical grounds. If the apparition is genuine it may come not from God but from the Devil to sow evil and disharmony among the faithful. If the apparition is no more than the imaginings of an illiterate girl – which Bernadette was – the Church will be brought into disrepute.

Bernadette's story was officially accepted and growing numbers of people came to visit the shrine set up in the grotto. Now, each year, more than six million pilgrims visit Lourdes, a small town in the foothills of the Pyrenees where this apparition is believed to have happened. About 52 of them have claimed a miraculous recovery, but the head of the Lourdes Medical Bureau finds only five of these merit serious investigation. He said in an interview 'This is a normal town. There aren't permanent miracles happening here... The truth is Heaven doesn't exist on earth.' Since

Bernadette had her vision some 150 years ago there have been 66 officially validated miraculous recoveries – each meticulously examined and recorded.

In Lourdes we stayed in a small hotel where I began to realise that there were expectations crowding round me. I was constantly told how lucky I was to be making this pilgrimage. I listened politely but I knew that nothing could cure me. My paralysed arm was due to my sinfulness in the convent. Indeed, I had been very lucky to have recovered the use of one arm. Preparations were made for me to visit the grotto where Bernadette believed – undoubtedly sincerely – that the Virgin Mary had appeared to her. The Virgin is a very important figure in the Catholic hierarchy; probably the focus of more prayers than her son Jesus or God Himself. It is believed that she has very powerful influence with both of them. The special focus of prayers to her is the Rosary, repeated in groups of five decades, often with the aid of beads, in times of distress, in life and at the hour of death. It was the first prayer I was taught in the convent. Since then I have always associated it with the heavy black beads and formidable crucifixes hanging at the waists of black clad nuns.

'Hail Mary full of Grace. The Lord is with thee and blessed is the fruit of the womb, Jesus. Holy Mary, Mother of God, pray for us sinners now and at the hour of our death. Amen.'

The morning came when I was dressed in a white cotton covering, put in a wheelchair and pushed by my mother, in a group of Glaswegians, down a hill to the grotto. High on the cliff wall above was a niche holding a large statue of the Virgin Mary, and below, looking up at her, a similar statue of Bernadette. I was taken out of the chair and lifted bodily by a brancardier – a man deputed to look after me – to be totally immersed in a pool of sacred water from the spring. I was aware that I carried into the water the expectations of my companions.

Nothing happened, nothing happened and nothing happened – except that I became very wet. I was immersed a second time – but still nothing happened. The group around me dispersed and my mother wheeled me back up the hill to the hotel. I knew I was a failure. I had let everyone down.

The following year they made me try again, this time without my mother. I was to travel with a small group of women, parishioners of St. Paul's church, across the Channel, and then by train across France. It was a very different experience – much more relaxed than going with my mother. The women weren't really interested in me; which suited me very well. On the train I saw for the first time, what I was to see a lot of later, the flirtatious interaction between priests and Catholic women. A small group of them – perhaps three – would sit round a table in the carriage, leaving free a seat in the aisle into which one of the younger priests would insert himself.

The women would begin to talk more loudly, giggle a lot and direct all their attention to him. He in turn responded warmly and jokily, safe in the numbers involved. He would never have been seen alone with one of them. It would be clear that they were all enjoying themselves enormously; the women enjoying this rare opportunity to be close to a priest, the priest enjoying the risky, slightly dangerous situation in a safe environment. I stood by the table of one group with fascination, not understanding what was going on but recognising the tension circulating in the group – standing beside the priest, watching and judging. My concentration was interrupted by the priest's hand sliding up my thigh under my school uniform. Many years later I wrote a poem.

A DIFFERENT PILGRIMAGE

Swaying through France
I walked through
pilgim laden carriages,
my paralysed arm
my credential
my badge of honour.
White socks,
school skirt,
ready for Lourdes
and a miracle cure.
My mother in Glasgow
praying.
Sitting in the aisle
he stopped me –
talking, asking,
who, why, when, where,
his hand on my thigh,
moving gently up my leg.
I said, 'Yes Father',
my body said, 'Yes, Father'
but he stopped at the elastic.
I knew he knew,
and he knew I knew
a different pilgrimage
had been offered me.

This second venture was no more successful than the first. I had not started out on either of these journeys with great expectations. My life so far had not given me much hope that the future would be better than the past. The losses tended to outweigh the gains, and I had settled into a state of acceptance of the world as it was. I had also learned how to adjust physically to having the use of only one arm. If I had any regret, it was for not being able to continue piano lessons. But I could read, and that became my escape route.

Three splendid years

The next three splendid years were enriched for me by my access to the local library and to Tollcross Park. The library had been opened in 1925, the year of my birth, by Mr. Montgomery, then Lord Provost. It had cost £21,000 and was one of what became known as the Carnegie Libraries. At first it provided only newspapers and books, but was graced by a splendid stained glass panel celebrating St. Mungo. This has been incorporated into the reconditioned library, which offers services beyond anything initially dreamed of. Even without these services this library in its initial simplicity offered me riches of information, ideas and imagination for which I have been eternally grateful, along with my gratitude to the elderly little nun who first taught me to read.

I had been three when my father left us, but there had been troubles long before that. I was suddenly cut off from him, from the smells and surfaces that were different from my mother's. I must have enjoyed them because when, much later, I found them in other men I sensed a recognition of pleasures lost. I soon lost her too. She went off to work as a midwife, leaving me with my grandmother – that plump, soft-skinned, peaceful, unimaginative woman who saved my life.

I had been plump too, but I became thin. I had been garrulous and became silent, a shadow hanging on to my grandmother's skirts. I knew that the world was dangerous. I knew that I was dangerous. I had destroyed my own world, and I was being punished. The nuns had taught me that. I pretended to be invisible. Sometimes I thought I *was* invisible, but then I would become frightened in case I disappeared altogether.

Quite often my mother would reappear and when she did there was always drama... Presents, high spirits, laughter and funny stories. My grandmother and my two aunts would forget the tempers, the hysteria, the self-pity, and they would respond, becoming an audience. The house would come alive, the fire burn more brightly, the gas lamp glow more lambently on the auburn hair, the blue eyes and the skin I am reminded of when I look at my pearls.

I would be re-enchanted every time and accept excuses for the absences, the ache, the confusion, the loss. I daren't ask where *he* was. That way lay the dragons of anger and madness. The face would change, grow ugly, words would stream out; words I didn't understand but knew the sense of would be hurled into every corner of the room, would curl round me like snakes, push themselves into my ears and down my throat. Lying in bed together, exhausted with her anger, she would push her nipple into my mouth and tell me to suck because she loved me. So I learned not to ask. Instead I listened. I listened hoping to hear something I could understand, to hear something I could hold in my hand,

When she was home we would sleep together in the hole in the wall bed in the room of my grandmother's room and kitchen.

But before going to sleep she would tell me about her work in a hospital, helping women to bring out the babies that had grown inside them. Before giving them to their mothers she had to wash them, dress them in long white clothes and cuddle them. It sounded lovely and she would tell me this while cuddling me and telling me how much she loved me – and how much she had suffered for me.

She was very explicit about the circumstances surrounding my occupying and leaving her womb and I was to hear about it in detail both then and later. The story as it unfolded in my childhood years seemed heavy with menace way beyond my understanding. As an adult I tried to piece it together. Their honeymoon, their first physical contact in those strict days, had been a disaster. She suffered from a hysterical contraction of the muscles of the vagina which made penetration impossible. One can only imagine my father's frustration. On their return home he consulted his doctor who performed an operation which involved cutting the vagina in a way that made it impossible for the muscles to contract.

The battle was won but the war was lost. From that point on sex was nauseous, disgusting, filthy behaviour that women had to suffer in order to have babies. It became a battleground on which they lacerated themselves for the next three years. My birth, ten months after that operation, must have contributed to the battle since I have it on her own authority that it was prolonged, painful, difficult and involved a crude incision with no anaesthetic. At this distance I can see how what had happened must have been very confusing for my father. I look now for excuses for him.

Meanwhile, my life was simple. Every morning I would be at the door of the library, waiting for it to open so that I could return the book I had taken out the previous day and choose a new one. If it was raining I would have to go back home and find time, privacy and a place to read. If the weather was tolerable I would head up Wellshot Road to Tollcross Park. Here I would find a seat, preferably down near the burn that ran through the park, and read. *(Kay and I visited that bench by the burn several times. I used to say that they should place a blue plaque on it to commemorate the child who sat reading there – and was sad when they removed it early in the twenty-first century.)* Usually finishing the book before going home for my dinner (nobody talked about 'lunch') I could change it for one that would keep me going for the rest of the day at home. *(Kay was the fastest reader I have known, and that must have started early.)*

The park was a delight. It wasn't impossibly huge, only 82 acres, and had been bought by Glasgow Corporation in 1897 for £29,000. It had belonged to the last of the Dunlop family who had owned the Clyde Ironworks and built a mansion house in the grounds. Designed by an Edinburgh architect, the mansion had cost more than the Corporation had paid for the whole estate. It had even had a deer park and the last red deer died there in 1911. Tollcross was seen as the aristocratic and exclusive part of Shettleston with which it didn't really want to be associated.

Her father returns

When I was ten a man entered our family without warning or explanation. I didn't know him. To her own family, my mother called him 'Mick'. That was a term of abuse, an Irish name, and I knew that Irish men were dirty, lazy drunkards. I was never actually told that. It was just something everyone knew, and certainly Mr. McElhoney, who lived in the single end in the close round the corner, fitted that picture.

In time I realised that 'Mick' was my father. I think I picked that up from my Gran and my aunts talking to each other. They never talked to me about him. To them he had been a great dark secret, spoken of in whispers, and never, ever, if my mother was around. He was the elephant in the room everyone pretended wasn't there. He was such a large elephant and it was such a tiny room so it was sometimes hard to keep up the pretence. I didn't really understand what a 'father' was. I knew no other children so had no access to ordinary families in which there were two parents. So it came as something of a shock to be told that we were going to live with this man about whom I had never heard a good word spoken, but about whom I had heard many bad words.

I hadn't been at school since the age of six and all I knew of the world was filtered to me through the day-to-day experiences of my grandmother, my two aunts and my mother. My mother's contribution came in those excruciating descriptions of the terrible things that had happened to her in her short experience of marriage, her hatred of 'Mick', and the occasional combination of fiendish temper and equally powerful and marvellous fun and gaiety allied to her pleasure at bringing babies into the world. What else I knew came from books.

I was to gain my first lesson in the confusing links between love and hatred. My father wanted a divorce. But letting him have that would mean, for my mother, losing him, probably to another woman. Divorce was a social disgrace – I had heard Mrs. Brown upstairs going on about that with my grandmother. But more important in our family was the fact that the Catholic Church forbad it – although I don't think that either of these things mattered to my mother. She wanted above all to hold on in any way possible to this man whom she loved with the most passionate and deadly intensity.

According to the legal conventions of the day, if he offered her 'bed and board' and she rejected that, he could sue for divorce. To his horror, I guess, she accepted. He had not understood that beneath her hatred of him was a deeper yearning to be loved by him, for she was still at some level in love with him in one of the many extraordinary meanings of that phrase. It was to be a situation full of tension, which I absorbed through my skin.

Reluctantly he rented a flat, ominously within a hundred yards of his mother, and installed us there. The experience of moving was life transforming. Instead of a crowded room and kitchen, in the close of a shabby building on a main road, we were to live in a relatively spacious top floor flat, in a very respectable area; not in a street but in a drive. I didn't fully appreciate the implication of an address which included the word 'drive' rather than 'street' until much later, although my mother was obviously pleased. The flat had three rooms, all of a reasonable size. We used one of them in common – a kitchen with a cooking stove and an open fire, where cooking and eating took place. We occasionally sat round the table together for an evening meal there. One I shared with my mother as a bedroom, and my father had his own bedroom. The difference in our life style was summed up in the fact that the lavatory was inside the house and not out on the stairs. In addition, its pan sat in a bathroom and there was really a bath there. My previous experience of baths had been confined to the Shettleston public baths, so this was a life changing experience, setting for me previously unimaginable standards.

But even more significant was the fact that we were sharing this house with a man who I was given to understand, without the words ever being said, was my father. All I knew about fathers came from books. In the children's section of the library they were not much in evidence but, when they were, they seemed kind, pleasant people. As I progressed into the adult section, where I struggled with Dickens and Maupassant, I gained a more confusing and complicated picture.

When I met him for the first time I fled back into my convent-acquired defence of distancing myself from what was happening to me. I had, and still have, no idea what he thought of me. The experience brought me an awed recognition of human complexity. Clearly this was to be a merely technical sharing of bed and board, but he began to take some responsibility for me. Most important, he insisted that I attend school – the local Protestant school.

My father took me to meet his mother, my previously unknown grandmother. She was a formidable lady, dressed from head to foot in black and spurning any change in her clothing from the late nineteenth century when she had grown up. I was aware of being looked up and down with distaste. No words of welcome or kindness were offered me although I had always known that my middle name of McIntosh was her birth name. I also met my grandfather, a shadowy figure in a chair, who seemed kind and gentle but took no part in decision making. She had brought up five sons on a tiny income, settling them all into good jobs and managing to get the youngest into university. She attended the most prestigious of the Protestant churches. All this was no mean achievement. To see one of her sons throw himself away on a Catholic must have been a bitter blow. I can understand why I might not have been welcome since I had, in a phrase of the day, bad blood in me.

I was taken on a series of visits to be introduced to various other members of the family, but on each occasion I was not allowed to wear the rather ugly prosthesis supporting my arm and had to put my left hand in my pocket to help mask my disability. It was rather overwhelming to realise that I was part of this large family. But more overwhelming, and quite disorienting, was the realisation that I was beginning to like my father. The phrase 'your father' had only ever been directed around me in anger or disgust. More often, my mother had called him 'Mick'. I never found out why – I don't think she knew herself – but it was a common degrading term of abuse directed at the Irish which my father, had he known it, would have deeply resented. I had been brought up to believe him wicked, untrustworthy, a liar and a disinterested father who had abandoned me. The fact that he had never asked to see me in all these years, not even when I was in hospital, sturdily reinforced that view. Now I was spending some time with this man and finding him thoughtful and interesting, albeit within the values of Glasgow's Protestant middle class. I was of course torn.

My mother's anger seemed undiminished, although there were nights when, supposed to be asleep, I could hear her plead with my father for physical love. Meanwhile she unwittingly helped me with my invisibility project. Our flat was diagonally across the street from that of my father's parents and I was enrolled as a spy to report whenever he made visits to them. Le Carré would have been proud of me. I learned to hide behind the curtains so that he wouldn't see me watching him, although he must have suspected what was happening because she couldn't help accusing him of plotting with his mother against her. She ruthlessly questioned me about his movements and every contact I had with him.

During these months I read like water running down a drain. Reading helps me to shut out the things I don't want to know or think about. But he didn't believe that I understood anything I read. He hadn't been there when I learned to read. We knew so little about each other. Before I got to sleep he rationed me to two pages of a children's book his brother had given me. I couldn't tell him that by the age of eight I had worked my way through the children's department of the Public Library where I spent my days. I was working my way through Maupassant when he reappeared in my life.

I knew the kind of little girl he wanted. I knew too that I could never be her. So I did my best to pretend to be what I was not. I had to be intelligent but not too sharp; obedient, respectful, loving, but not embarrassingly so; always ready to agree to his suggestions but not make any of my own. Most important, I must not be a cripple, but I could do nothing about that. At that point the pretence cracked. I *was* a cripple – I had heard him telling my mother I was. He was the first person to name me in that way. 'Take that thing off her arm' he had said before taking me to visit his family. 'I don't want to be seen with a cripple'. But I desperately wanted to be close to him. I don't know why.

For some years now my body had played an important part in my life. Important but detached. Ever since my paralysis I had in some sense been detached from it. The last time I remembered being fully connected with it was when, running down Shettleston Road at the age of four, my knickers were filled with shit. That was real; as was my grandmother's loving cleansing ritual. Her total acceptance of my body, in whatever state she found it, brought together all aspects of myself. But that had not lasted long before I was banished to the convent.

The head of the school I was to go to rejected me. My mother exploded when she got a letter from the Director of Education, a Mr. Mackintosh, telling her that I would be allocated to 'a school for children who are mentally and physically handicapped'. A whirlwind of activity followed. I was pushed into a coat and hustled down the road to a tram going to Bath Street where the Education Offices occupied a splendid Victorian building. I was marched through the great front door; a brief encounter with a receptionist revealed where the Director's office could be found and I was dragged up a splendid staircase and marched – hauled would be a better word – past secretaries and officials straight into the Director's office and pushed in front of him. He was then subjected to a stream of anger, which described in detail how ashamed he ought to be to suggest even for a minute that this child he saw in front of him should be exposed to the humiliation and horror of a school for the Mentally and Physically Handicapped. I can't remember any of the words but I remember the tone exactly. I am convinced also from memories of a host of similar outbursts that the beautiful wavy auburn hair and flashing turquoise eyes were making the impression I had so often seen on men's faces as they encountered her. I shut down as I so often did and my next memory is of starting at the school that had rejected me.

There were problems. I was at first put into a class with the five-year-olds. It probably seemed sensible. Although my basic education had been interrupted for four years I was ahead of my age group in everything you can learn from a public library. But that left gaps. Although a fast and fluent reader, writer and speller, I had only the sketchiest glimmerings of arithmetic, multiplication or long division. I knew the months of the year but not the numbers that represented them. I didn't even know my alphabet.

(She never did, to the end of her life. Nor did she know her multiplication tables.) So I was seen as an oddity, both in the classroom and in the playground. I didn't fit into any known category either for the children or the teachers. This impression was fed not only by my disability but also by my lack of conventional schooling. It became obvious that I didn't understand the Protestant rituals and hymns with which the day started, and it emerged that I was a Catholic. Glasgow's Protestants saw Catholics, who were usually of Irish origin, as inferior human beings, and I was a scapegoat for all the prejudices my classmates had acquired from their parents.

I had a somewhat similar problem in a milder form. The only Protestant I had known was the formidable Mrs. Brown who lived on the top flat above my grandmother. When I met my father's equally formidable mother I recognised the same qualities in the two women: a toughness and a conviction of their own rectitude. I knew from my experiences in street processions that Protestants hated Catholics, believing them to be socially inferior worshipers of idols – the statues in Catholic chapels – and to be loyal only to the Pope. It was Reformation language.

Many years later Kay recalled these memories in a poem.

EXPERIENCE OF TWO SCHOOLS IN THE WEST OF SCOTLAND

The Convent School	The Protestant School
Bad blood in you	Bad blood in you
They said.	They said.
Your father's a Protestant.	Your mother's a Catholic.
He'll go to hell.	She'll go to hell.

You won't get to heaven	You'll never be trusted.
Not with bad blood	Catholics are bad
They said.	They said.
Then I understood	Then I understood
Why	Why
The nuns hated me.	The teachers pitied me.

I tried
To cut myself
To get rid of
The blood.

I had learned somehow or other that Catholics were not supposed to read the Bible. It was a sin to do so. Yet here was I in a Protestant school with a Bible I had to carry every day in my schoolbag. The issue of the Bible flared up one evening. I had come home from school to find my mother even more tense than usual. I sat quietly at the kitchen table to do my homework, my schoolbag emptied beside me. When my father came in she wasted no time in turning her fury on him and – unusually, because he normally walked away from confrontation – he responded angrily. Before I knew what was happening, the frying pan on the stove was thrown at him and my Bible picked up from the table and thrown on to the fire. A diatribe on its heretical character followed.

I had to go to school the following morning without my Bible and make excuses for not having it. It was at this stage of my life that I was learning to tell believable lies. I knew that telling lies was a sin and that if I died during the night I would go to Hell, but that was a better option than telling the truth in that friendless classroom. I cannot now recall what lie I invented but

I do remember that the following evening my father replaced my Bible.

I don't know if this experience was a turning point for him but it wasn't long before he disappeared. We never saw each other again. *(That was how she remembered it; but her daughter Sheena tells me it was not quite true. Long after, in the 1960s, he returned briefly from Southern Rhodesia to Glasgow and they met twice.)*

I was left with one powerful memory. Lying in bed one night when I was ten years old I listened to my mother in the next room trying to seduce him. She pleaded with him to make love to her, offering her breast and body in the most explicit terms. He rejected her, wearily rather than unkindly. She collapsed in floods of tears and threats of suicide. The following Sunday – I vividly remember the stillness of the outside world – before any of us were dressed she told me to go in to my father's room and get into bed with him. I was reluctant, but she was insistent and I saw no alternative. He had been sleeping and was surprised to be wakened to find me there. I desperately wanted to be close to him. I don't know why. He stirred and turned towards me and I stretched my body along his – close to him. He turned away sharply and, without a word being said, I knew I had done something wrong. It was to be years before I understood what his response meant. To me it was simply another rejection. I would have let him do whatever he wanted with my body. I suppose I should be grateful that he turned away.

The experiences I was having during these months leave scars in the psyche that are as real as physical scars – scars that may last a lifetime.

Seventy years later Kay and I were sitting in a cinema together when I realised that she was crying. When we got home she wrote a poem.

FORGOTTEN LONGING

In the film
the dying actor said
'Come to me my daughter'
and I found myself weeping.
What does it mean to find your *self* weeping?
In my weeping
I found what I had lost...
The forgotten longing for a father
who might have said
'Come to me, my daughter'.

A reflection

Later in life, when working with young women who had been
involved in incestuous sexual relationships with their fathers, my
early experience helped me to understand that what the outside
world calls abuse was sometimes seen by the girls involved as
the only source of affection and attention in their lives. I have
learned that if a father transfers his attention to a younger sister
this can create agonies of jealousy and rejection. I don't know
what happens with boys but that must have its own dynamic. I am
grateful to my father for not taking advantage of my neediness.
I won't say innocence because I think unhappy and emotionally
abused children (as distinct from sexually abused) have a constant
underlying knowledge of what they need: a feeling of being loved
and cared for, with physical – preferably skin-to-skin – contact.

Emotional abuse is not taken as seriously as sexual abuse or physical abuse, but it should be. While those practices are horrible and damaging, at least they can be clearly identified and given a specific and recognisable name. But emotional abuse is made up of an unremitting series of separate, sometimes quite small, undramatic situations, which eat away at the self-esteem, self-respect and self-worth of the child. The most common weapon is humiliation. This may be inflicted by parents, or by a teacher or fellow pupils. It may not be recognised that these experiences can leave scars in the psyche as real as physical scars. Without healing opportunities they can last for a lifetime.

Her mother

She and I struggled on. I missed him. He had brought a new dimension into my life, a realisation that there was a big world out there – other countries, other ways of living. I realise now that I quite liked him and found him interesting. I could never have shared these thoughts with my mother so I became even more impenetrable. She had regaled me with stories about him going off to enjoy himself at Catterick in the Territorial Army. He clearly had a passion for the army in which he had served during the First World War, but she saw these Territorial weekends as opportunities for him to 'go with' other women. I never understood what this phrase meant, but I can now appreciate that it must have been difficult for her, caring for an infant while he swanned off, looking handsome in army uniform. She was a woman who needed constant attention and affirmation of her attractiveness.

With my father gone, my mother and I left the posh 'Drive' and returned to Shettleston and a room and kitchen in a 'Street'. It had an inside lavatory but no bath. I had reached an age and a stage where this mattered. We brought with us the furniture my mother had bought for her marriage. It had been with me all my life – an overblown, dramatically covered sofa with matching armchairs and the upright piano had particular significance for me. I had had chicken pox on that sofa, wept on it and dreamt on it. The piano stool had been my desk. Before the polio I had tried to play the piano, and again afterwards with one hand till I had to give up. My mother played it erratically, vamping furiously with her left hand and singing lovely, maudlin, sentimental songs.

But all that was now over. She set about committing suicide with the aid of alcohol – a slow method and one whose meaning I didn't understand but whose practice was intolerable. My father was never again mentioned. With his final departure the meaning seemed to have gone out of her life. But I still have on my walls some of the mirrors and charming artefacts that were with her till she died, as a reminder of the woman she might have been if her life had taken a different path.

I was transferred to a convent school with the name of Our Lady and St. Francis. My life became set in a bleak pattern. It was another school in which I felt quite alien. Noone was openly unkind. I was no longer wearing the arm brace, and I was getting better at disguising my inability to use my left arm. Although I never quite fitted in, I was becoming more skilled at managing that.

We established a routine of sorts. I became highly practised in the art of concealing everything about my inner life – even from the exquisite golden girl who set about seducing me, until her attention was diverted by the gym teacher who seduced her. In spite of my intimate knowledge of the birth processes and the infinite variety of venereal infections I was radiantly innocent of the complexities of love. My seducer awakened what seemed to me a new set of possibilities. Together we explored love poetry, she constantly seeking to extend the boundaries of her own experience; me watching, as I was to do so often later in life, watching but not quite belonging – wanting to share in this clearly commanding passion.

I had extraordinary freedom. Where I went, who I was with, how I spent my time were never questioned. My mother had a fierce inner life, which left little room for anyone else. For many years I had not sought her attention, finding it more of a burden than a comfort or a resource. I could stay in and read: she would never question what I read. I could go out at night, alone, to the cinema: she would never ask what I had seen or with whom. I would take an afternoon off school simply to wander: she never knew. (*Kay must have been living a quite hazardous life. She was taught, she told me, never to approach a policeman when roaming the streets at night. They were dangerous. Catholic working class girls lived in a different city from that experienced by middle class men.*)

On the other hand there were evenings, sometimes days, when I was cornered and the waves of my mother's madness poured over me. They were always triggered by an encounter with someone who she felt had insulted her, but they seldom stayed there. Her rage and pain would progress to a long practised explosion of hatred against my father and everything to do with him – particularly his sexual habits. I tried in every way to avoid being dragged in as another focus for her rage. But no matter what I said or didn't say, no matter what mask I tried to mold on my face, the point would come when she turned on me simply because I was there.

I learned to cope with that over the years. I could retreat quite quickly within myself and leave my body, uninhabited by my consciousness, to watch what was going on. What I never learned to cope with was the next stage when, with eyes shifting wildly from side to side, she would suddenly stop and not speak again. She would move briskly about her ordinary affairs without saying a word to me about anything. We would eat in silence, go to bed and get up in silence, but under the silence there was a brooding energy that filled the room. All my life she had done this both to her mother and to me. To have my existence denied in this way was desperately painful.

I was increasingly having to cope with the new woman my mother had become. That gay, slightly manic, upwardly motivated, infuriating but entrancing woman had disappeared to be replaced by a rather depressed person, frequently in bed at five o'clock when I came home from school. Her earlier tendency to drink when under pressure had escalated till she was increasingly out of touch with my reality. There was no one with whom I could have shared my distress about her behaviour. She had great skills in presenting herself to the world for short periods of time. When the call came in the middle of the night for her help as a midwife she could pull on her uniform and sally forth apparently sober. She did not bother to deceive me, but she was embarrassed if I was with her when she needed to buy drink. I would have to wait outside the wine shop.

WAITING IN THE CAFE

Saturday afternoon
under Cental Station bridge
there is a cafe.
A narrow stair winds
upwards from the door
to a balcony with
little marble tables.
This child sat there
waiting, waiting.
For you. Waiting
and wondering
but knowing and dreading.
You came, the familiar
smell of perfumed powder
and sweet wine
like incense before
you. Your bones
are dust now. My own
will soon be laid to rest.
But I remember as if
it were yesterday.

Then fate brought me an escape from helplessness and guilt.

III

ESCAPE

On that Sunday morning in September, after mass, we listened to Neville Chamberlain on the radio and the declaration of war. My mother exploded with excitement. Until a few months earlier she had been a fervent supporter of Hitler and Mussolini, partly as a bulwark against communism, which was the official line of the Catholic Church, but also because at some level she was excited by the drama of their style. If we had lived in Germany she would have been a fervent Nazi. Now the drama of patriotism overwhelmed her. The Daily Express published a map along with a supply of different coloured pins to represent the Allied Forces. This was prominently displayed and for several weeks kept meticulously up to date, but then enthusiam waned.

Part of the reason for this waning was the appointment of our downstairs neighbour as the ARP (Air Raid Precautions) Warden for our building. She was a formidable lady who diverted the energy previously used to terrorise her meek husband into a determination that no chink of light from our building would guide the German Air Force to Glasgow. This empowered her to bully and threaten anyone who didn't take her as seriously as she took herself. To my mother she was like a red rag to a bull. Like everyone else, we had bought yards of dull black cotton and made them into curtains which had to be fitted over our windows. My mother's sewing, like all her house keeping accomplishments, was creative but slapdash. Before long we had to supplement the stitches with safety pins, but each failure was drawn to our attention with an intensive energy, which, if available to the Chiefs of Staff, would have ended the war in a fortnight.

Air raid shelters appeared in the back courts, one to each close. When the air raids began we were supposed to go and sit in them, knee to knee, wrapped in shawls and blankets. After one experience I refused to go back. I began to make contact with my subtle yearning that my existence should cease. Not that I sought death: the nuns had taught me that death did not bring an end to existence. But I began to wonder if being killed by a bomb might cause such disintegration of my body that it would be a step on the way to oblivion. It was oblivion I sought.

I was alone most of the time. Along with her work as a midwife my mother had taken on various voluntary duties, some of which kept her out overnight. Air raids came and went and I would either do my homework through them, or sleep through them. Once I was turned out of the cinema in the middle of a film and had to walk disconsolately home down dark back lanes to avoid being shoved into a shelter by an officious warden.

The war seemed to keep my mother's madness and drinking in check. Neither had disappeared but they were driven undergound, emerging in shorter, less intense and less destructive episodes. I felt I was having a breathing space and out of that breathing space came a thin thread of self-preservation. The Government had made plans for the evacuation of children from cities that were likely to be targets for the bombers. Glasgow would obviously be one of them. They were to be cared for by families living in safer country places. There was a sense of excitement everywhere. One day all the girls in my school were told to take a letter to their parents asking them if they wanted us to be evacuated. Taking mine home, it only occurred to me as I was about to give it to my mother that I might have some choice in the matter. Without knowing where the words came from, I told her 'We all have to be evacuated. You have to sign this letter.' I don't remember any protest from her. Like so many others, she was excited by the drama of war. This was my first major betrayal and my first serious attempt to save myself. *(Kay was still only thirteen years old when she made this life-changing decision.)*

Evacuee

Evacuation began in September 1939. In three days, 120,000 children left Glasgow. Scenes at the railway stations were chaotic with crowds of children and their parents struggling in fear and tears to find the right trains, many wanting to change their minds at the last minute. I had no such wish. Nor, it seemed, had my mother. I left with a group of about forty girls from my school, clearly identifiable in our brown uniforms. No nuns came with us. We were in the care of three lay teachers. The train started and we were ultimately turned out at the village of Closeburn about ten miles north of Dumfries and walked a hundred yards down the road to Wallace Hall Academy where I was to continue my precarious involvement in education.

For most evacuees this was to be a disastrous experience. They went home as soon as they could. I cannot, surely, have been the only one for whom it was a relief to be away from home – the only one who needed space and an escape from pain? I was lucky to have this opportunity in a way that preserved the pretences and the masks. Other children have to run away or to seek escape inside their heads by taking drugs or sniffing glue. Once away from my mother I shut her out of my head, opening myself up to the new experiences that would flood in upon me. I would never be the same again.

At Closeburn we were in the heart of the Scottish countryside. The school, a brown stone building of classic design, had been founded by John Wallace, a Glasgow merchant and a native of Closeburn. He had left £1,600 in 1723 to build the Academy – very much in the tradition of Scottish commitment to education and loyalty to one's birthplace. (The school has now been transferred to the small town of Thornhill nearby. In 2005 it was given the Schools of Ambition Award and ranked fifth among state schools in Scotland. John Wallace would have been proud.) We gathered in the assembly hall of the school, a pathetically small group, and I was sent with an older girl to a chicken farm two miles up the road on a low hill above the River Nith.

Chickens and Pigs

This was a revelation. I had only seen a dead chicken – and that very rarely. Here I saw hundreds running around an open field. They were penned up overnight to protect them from predators and their eggs were collected next day. I was enchanted with them and with learning to drink whipped raw egg. The farm was run by a young couple who were, I think, relieved to find two reasonably polite and well behaved young people as their guests. Within a month, most of our fellow pupils had returned to Glasgow, and after that a steady trickle of the remainder followed them. This seems to have been the nationwide pattern. Soon we two were the only evacuees left. (I regret I cannot recall my companion's name. Separated by a year or two in age, we were never very close.)

My mother sent me brief letters and regular pocket money, but it was while I was on the chicken farm that she wrote to say she would come to visit me one Saturday. I do not know what inspired that visit. I had no clue from her letters whether she was missing me or if my absence was a relief, but she must have had some reason for making the three-hour bus journey. I was filled with apprehension, not knowing which mother to expect but hoping desperately for the enchanting, loving figure who could move my heart with joy and pity.

I was waiting at the bus stop. As she stepped down, one glance at the flush on the cheeks, the subtle slackness of the facial muscles, the slightly foolish smile, together with the lavish toilet water scent enveloping me in her dramatic embrace were enough to tell me it was going to be a bad time. As the bus drew away we stood looking at each other. In spite of my regular letters my mother couldn't have imagined what she was coming to. She was dressed for a city outing with high-heeled shoes, and an elegant green coat and hat framing her auburn hair. There was the crocodile handbag which I knew from experience would hold a half bottle of something or other. The village street had one small shop and half a dozen houses. I lived a mile and a half away along country lanes – and in any case I couldn't bear to take her there.

Had I been older, with more experience of the world, I would have bundled her back on the bus as soon as I saw her and together we could have travelled another twelve miles to the town of Dumfries where we could have found an anonymous cafe where we could sit until it was time for her to go home. But children don't have these skills and are caught in the world that adults make for them. Moreover, my act of rebellion in getting away from Glasgow was, as I saw it, an act of betrayal that had exhausted my resources for dealing with her.

It would be two hours before a bus came to take her away, and there was nothing we could do but walk around in a vague sort of way. She had had enough to drink not to be too critical of me, but I knew that she would have to find some privacy to top up if her fuddled sweetness was to hold out and not turn into irritability. We started up the road to the river and I did my best to talk in an interesting way about the school, the village and my life. That failed to gain much response so I began to ask questions about Glasgow, my grandmother and my aunties. Her replies were still vague and suddenly she said she needed to pass water. I took her into a field, which had a thick hedge, and said I would go back into the road and keep watch in case anyone came. The road was in fact deserted in all directions. There were in any case few cars and little petrol for the few there were. She came back smiling cheerfully and more talkative, but only a quarter of an hour had passed.

Somehow or other we stumbled through the rest of our time. She had the advantage of her protective alcoholic haze. I had, as so often with her, a jumble of feelings: love, anger, protectiveness, but mostly a sense of helplessness. With no excuses to drink, her haze soon turned to sullenness and we headed back to the village where we stood in silence waiting for the bus to take her away – my whole self drenched with a sense of guilt and failure.

Suddenly she went in to the shop and asked if she could use their lavatory. By this time I had given up and simply waited passively. It was the time of day when a few local men would gather in the shop to discuss the news. I had always been shy of going in at that time because of the strong male bonds I sensed as soon as I entered. A few minutes later I heard roars of laughter and when I put my head round the door I could see my mother, the centre of everyone's attention, smiling, beautiful and flirtatious, brought back to life by the fix of alcohol she had taken in the lavatory and the attention she was getting. My relief was enormous, and when the bus came I helped her on to it, babbling cheerfully and promising to write. But I knew I never wanted her to visit me again.

I was not unhappy all the time. I was constantly learning new things about the way people lived. The men in the shop always remembered my mother and her capacity for charming them. Some of that glow passed on to me so the shop became a place where, even if I didn't contribute to the conversation, I was welcome to stay and listen. It was the only place resembling a club the village had and in the evenings there was always a group of men exchanging news and ideas. The most stunning occasions were when one would start reciting a poem, usually from Burns, and like a swallow catching midgies the reference would be taken up by another and another, and for an hour or more I would stand listening entranced, not only to Burns but to Shelley, Byron and Keats.

The tone of their discussions was radical and democratic, breathing a sort of libertarian dislike of privilege – in particular a dislike of the abuse of privilege. For me this fitted in well with my dawning political consciousness. Before I had left Glasgow, I got to know one of my mother's patients who had become a friend of hers and had taken a child refugee from a Republican family during the Spanish Civil War. Through her I had learned that my mother's pro-fascist postures had little justification. When I was evacuated she offered to send me regular copies of the

Independent Labour Party paper, *Forward*, which I was reading each week. This powerful little paper, with its roots in Christian Socialism with a Marxist gloss, blended amazingly well with the sturdy Scottish radical vision.

But my most healing experiences were the long walks to and from school along deserted country lanes. For a town child the coming and going of the seasons was a revelation. My senses were stirred as never before by the bird song, the smells, the wind – even the rain and thunder. It was on one of these walks that the first glimpse of future peace came to me. From my earliest years I had been constantly told that life was eternal, that death was merely a transition between the life we knew and the life hereafter. The life hereafter was divided into four possibilities: Limbo, Purgatory, Heaven or Hell. Limbo I knew I would never see, because that was reserved for babies who had not sinned but had not been baptised. I, to my embarrassment, had been baptised twice, once in the Protestant church and later, at my mother's request, when she left my father and returned to the Catholic Church. That was, for her, my proper baptism.

Purgatory I saw as a waiting room for Heaven in which ordinary souls waited patiently to be admitted to Heavenly bliss. Over the years I had made a significant contribution to the swifter passage of some souls by offering prayers, making sacrifices and lighting candles. This was very generous of me since my existential guilt made it unlikely that I would ever get to Heaven. My assumption had always been that I was destined for Hell. It was this thought that inhibited my wish for death. The thought that my consciousness of existence was doomed to go on forever was bad enough, but that it should do so while also suffering the most hideous torments was still for me a fact of life and death.

One day, walking peacefully down a lane between trees, I experienced the first of what I was later to recognise as a peak experience. I was transported outside my body, watching myself walk down the road and realising with a stunning conviction that this was it. My life would end and that would really be the end. As the two parts of me came together again I was exalted with happiness and relief. I could face carrying on if I knew that one day it would end. Sounds were sharper, colours were brighter, and I felt transformed as if I had made a bargain with fate.

The young woman of the chicken farm became pregnant and decided to ask for our removal. There had been no overt difficulties between us but she and her husband were probably happy to have a respectable reason for getting their home back for themselves. They would need our room as a nursery. My companion now decided that she too would go home, and I found myself the only evacuee who had chosen to stay. Only force could have made me sacrifice this period of amnesty. I knew the war would some day end and I would have to go home. But in some mysterious way I also knew that I couldn't risk going back yet.

I was transferred to The Rigg, a pig farm some three miles from the school. That meant a long walk every morning and evening, but I loved it. I particularly loved the pigs. I watched them being fed, having their litters and feeding their young. They had a quality of earthiness, of primaeval belonging, that reassured me and aroused my envy. They made me wonder if human consciousness was worth the price we pay for it. Might it not be better to have been born a simpler creature? I could find few arguments for being human. Their only disturbing characteristic was their habit of eating their children, but that seemed to me not very different from human behaviour. They have continued to fascinate me ever since: I don't know why. I was sorry to leave them when I was transferred yet again although I was glad to be spared the three-mile walk to school.

I asked Kay how she had got on with the other youngsters in her school. She said they had welcomed her – and particularly when the time for examinations came round. On one of these occasions, during the night before the exams, some boys hoisted her on their shoulders and pushed her through a high window of the school. Once inside, she had found the exam papers in an office, climbed out with copies of them and rejoined the boys. They found a quiet place where she took them through the questions and told them the answers. They got very good marks that year.

The original contract with the pig farmers was to care for me for a year. When that time came to an end the farmer's wife was willing to keep me on. But I increasingly felt that I was being used as a member of the family, serving the needs of the farm. I had learnt how to make cream and churn the butter, help with the pigs and pluck a fowl, but I knew that was not going to be my life. I needed more space in which to read and think than that busy extrovert family would tolerate. The Registration Officer agreed to find somewhere else for me and, on a temporary basis, I was transferred to the Manse where the minister's wife had so far managed to avoid having any evacuees.

The Manse

Living with them I began to understand why. She was engaged in a desperate rearguard action to prevent outsiders realising that her husband was sinking into madness. In a way I was familiar with, the subject most dreaded was never talked about. I liked him so much. He was a gentle creature who spent most of his day at the piano in the music room inventing small tunes, which he would play over and over again. His wife would rout him out on Sunday mornings to take a service. In those pre-ecumenical days, as a Roman Catholic I was not allowed to set foot in a Protestant church, but I would have liked to go there with him. The village gossiped constantly about him and his wife, and I was told that his congregation had shrunk to four faithful women who would not desert him, no matter how bizarre his sermons became.

His wife, perhaps to compensate, was hyperactive. She had one middle-aged woman from the village to help her with the housework and cooking, and by organising the household rigorously she managed to stay out of the house most of the day, working with the W.V.S. who kept her supplied with petrol for their essential journeys. The villagers were sceptical. She was known to prefer the company of the gentry to that of the farmers and saw herself as one of them – which she probably was.

The style of housekeeping, I realised later, was more upper middle than middle class. The Manse was a large, pre-Victorian house, more like an English vicarage than traditional Presbyterian. I was given a bedroom belonging to their son who was in the navy, in which I found, to my delight, a wider collection of modern prose and poetry than I had ever encountered. I used to lie in bed and read his books and wonder what he was like, this young man who had the complete works of Noel Coward and the poems of Auden and Spender.

I was treated as a house guest, but the family guarded their privacy by giving me a small study as well as a bedroom so we never needed to encounter each other except at meal times. These were a revelation to me. We ate in the dining room at a long table, always beautifully prepared. Breakfast was served on the side board and I was introduced to Oxford marmalade, which raised my standards of what to expect of breakfasts. Food was plentiful because the custom of bringing gifts to the minister survived his increasing neglect of his parish. Despite wartime rationing, we were never short of butter, cream, chicken, and a leg of lamb or pork.

I could have stayed there forever. The life style met all my needs. I could watch without being involved, I was cared for without having to make any emotional return, I had space within which I could explore my own mental boundaries. It was also aesthetically very satisfying. I encountered good linen, beautiful cutlery, polished wood, furniture which, without knowing why, I found to be right and fitting, and physical spaces that made appropriate settings for people to use and enjoy those things.

It couldn't last. The minister 's fragile hold on reality began to disintegrate from one day to the next. Still nothing was said, but it was clear there was a crisis in the air. It came suddenly. The car, filled with the petrol provided only for essential war work, became essential for the minister's wife to take her husband away. No one ever found out where they went: she came back only to supervise the removal of their household goods. The day she left I was reallocated to what was to be my last retreat from the world.

Trigony

I must have been assessed as being able to behave properly because I was now taken to the grandest house in the neighbourhood. It had been built in 1938 by Mrs. Dickson, a splendid lady who had sold her previous even grander house and large estate to a national enterprise that turned them into a convalescent home. Her new home was to be her hand-crafted equivalent of a dower house, only large enough for herself, her servants and a few guests. Trigony it was called; now a small, luxurious hotel. (*It still is. Kay and I visited it, were kindly received by its owners, and found the house and its garden very little changed since her childhood.*) It was a jewel; designed by Mrs Dickson and her architect with loving care and fitted with every modern device to be found in the most recent London Ideal Homes exhibition. If the Manse had enlarged my experience, this house was to shift it into a different category altogether.

I was given the suite Mrs Dickson had designed for her grandchildren, so I had a bedroom, a sitting room and a private bathroom. I was given the run of a wonderful library. The messages I had begun to hear at the Manse about the importance of form over content were strongly reinforced. The evening meal we had together I quickly learned to call 'dinner' rather than 'tea'. Three courses were compulsory, although on most occasions the first course was only an Oxo cube dissolved in hot water and served as soup. The bell under her foot would be pressed at the end of each course and the cook would come in to clear the plates before serving the next course. The dining room itself was a miracle of 1930s art nouveau with molded coves and concealed lighting, cream panelled walls and an oval table of pale wood. The tablemats were made up of small mirrored squares. Only the beautiful heavy silver came from an earlier era.

The dining room was linked to the drawing room by shuttered doors across its width and after dinner we would walk through to the morning room at the other end, which had the same shuttering. This meant that on grand occasions the whole length of that side of the house could be opened up. The drawing room and the morning-cum-sitting room had retained the style of Mrs.

Dickson's former home except that the drawing room was more elegant, the morning room cosier. In the drawing room, the piano and many other surfaces were covered with photographs in silver frames of weddings, studio portraits and signed photographs of the Royal Family. Over the time I lived in that house, her light, upper class voice gave me a running description of each person and the history of each photograph.

Mrs. Dickson was an Episcopalian, the Scottish version of an Anglican. I hadn't realised until then that there were any religions other than Roman Catholicism, Protestantism and Paganism. Once a month her splendid Daimler would be brought out of the garage and she would be driven to church in Dumfries. When she came back her clothes would be changed and what she had been wearing laid out in her dressing room for pressing before being replaced in her clothes cupboard. This was a daily routine for everything she wore.

I was now fifteen and living a more relaxed life than I had ever known – apart from my visits home at Christmas, Easter and in the summer; all painful and all as brief as I could make them. Mrs. Dickson's domestic staff were reduced to a cook-housekeeper, a village girl to help her, and the gardener-chauffer, but she maintained the style of the chatelaine of the great house in which she had spent most of her life. This was the genuine upper class article and I watched her as if she was a member of some strange tribe. I was trying to make sense of what I saw in the light of my increasing interest in the class struggle so vividly written about in the *Forward* newspaper I was reading. To me she could not have been more considerate or more charming while at the same time showing a total lack of interest in my personal affairs.

I was classed as superior to the servants so was expected to have dinner with her every evening unless she had guests. Mostly I went straight to my room afterwards, but occasionally I was invited into her small sitting room for coffee and to listen to the radio until the programme closed down. We would stand solemnly for the national anthem before saying goodnight with the formality that governed our relationship. Fortunately my republicanism had not yet reached the stage where I would have felt my integrity threatened by standing for 'God Save the King'.

I was introduced to a range of behaviour, most of which seemed entirely sensible, but all of it based on the assumption that there would be other people to do whatever needed to be done but wouldn't be done by oneself. My exploration of the iniquities of the class system and the class struggle was quite undeveloped. Everyone in the Dickson household seemed content and at ease with their lot. Certainly the cook-housekeeper was devoted to her mistress, with whom she had made the transition from great domestic responsibilities to this small domain. I was given a shadowy sense of what that must have been like.

The rule of the house was, 'A Place for Everything, and Everything in its Place'. After breakfast in her room and a leisurely but impeccable toilet, Mrs Dickson went to her small sitting room, which she called the morning room. There she discussed all the day's arrangements with the cook and the gardener. Menus for the day were decided – in this house very much within the restrictions of rationing. Her back and morals were rigid with patriotism and integrity, but the cook would quietly supplement their diet from the produce of local farms. That could not have been easy, and must have exercised her skills of accountancy because every item of expenditure had to be accounted for weekly.

Groceries were delivered from the nearest small town each week and there was a fixed rule that the account was settled when it reached the amount of five pounds. For the first time in my life I saw a cheque book and I was initiated into the mysteries of interest and capital. Goodness knows how it had got there, but I had found in the school library a two-volume copy of Karl Marx's *Capital* which, in bewilderment, I was trying to read. Mrs Dickson's constant monologue whenever we were together about rules of living for the upper classes taught me much more about economics than I was learning from its pages.

There was a time when Kay was planning to write an autobiography. Early drafts for this have enabled me to weave her recollections together into a fairly coherent story. But from this point onwards she neither wrote her life story nor did she talk much about it to me or to friends and relatives whom I have consulted. The pages that follow will consist of selections from writing she did for many different purposes over a long life. Since she rarely dated her work they may not appear in chronological order. Although she brought her experience to bear in everything she wrote, there will be no strong autobiographical thread on which the rest of this collection can be strung. Readers will have to decide for themselves which pages they want to read. Her poems will continue to appear occasionally but most of those included in this book will be brought together in Part X.

IV

PEACE ACTIVIST

Kay was an active member of a women's peace group. Starting with demonstrations, held several times a year at the gates and fences of the great nuclear submarine bases at Faslane and Coulport, often in alliance with the Campaign for Nuclear Disarmament and other peace groups, they soon extended into Scotland's cities and smaller towns – marching with drums, speaking, leafleting, and staging wittily and beautifully designed Punch and Judy shows in which an arms dealer selling competing bombs to Punch and the crocodile played a central part. In their early years, before the fences became impregnable to hand-held clippers, they broke into the bases to plant potatoes and bulbs 'to reclaim the land for the people'. A couple of policemen sent to arrest them caustically described the women as 'a fine lot of horticulturalists'. Thereafter, they took 'The Faslane Horticuturalists' – or 'The Horts' for short – as their title. These exploits inspired some of Kay's columns for New Society magazine. Also, a poem she wrote about one of the young women she met at the Peace Camp.

FASLANE

In dungarees,
nails gnawed
to quick,
Medusa hair,
unquiet eyes, she talked
of tits and cunts
and liberation.

Saints & Sinners, New Society, Vol. 60, 1982, p.343

This weekend is the first anniversary of the founding of the Ullapool branch of CND. Not, you might think, an event of great importance. Many people have never heard of Ullapool, let alone visited it. That is their loss. Apart from its own beauty, it is a gateway to the Western Isles. A boat leaves daily for the magical island of Lewis where 4,000 years ago the great standing stones of Callanish were placed in careful alignment with the sun, moon and stars.

When Jean Urquhart of Ullapool decided to start a CND branch she wanted a celebratory march to get it off to a good start. It wouldn't be an Aldermarston, but the port has two long streets, one along the harbour and one parallel to it. Wanting to do everything correctly, she consulted the local policeman about the route.

'Mistress Urquhart', he said, using the local mode of speech, 'How many people would you be expecting?' Jean hesitantly explained, 'It could be six or sixty.'

'I'll tell you what', he replied, 'it's my day off. But seeing it's yourself, I'll come and bring my car. If you have sixty people I'll lead the way and clear the streets. If there's six of you, I'll give you a lift.'

In the event, there were over a hundred. The sun blazed down and a piper led us. By walking slowly we spun the march out to last fifteen minutes before coming together in the village hall. In the evening in the Ceilidh Place, good food and drink, a jazz band and good company made it a great night for us all.

On stormy nights, I have remembered Ullapool in the sun. The Minch, the piece of water it overlooks, is one of the stormiest in the world. Gales blow up dramatically and cut Lewis and Harris off. A boat, called *The King's North Fisher*, regularly ploughs down the Minch, carrying plutonium waste from Dounreay to Windscale. It used to come by train, but after part of a consignment had accidentally been left overnight in a railway siding in Stirling, the change to a sea route was made. We all hope a sudden gale doesn't cause a greater disaster.

The Scots can hardly be blamed for seeing themselves as the nuclear waste bin of this less than totally United Kingdom. 'You don't keep pigs until you find out where you're going to put the shit' was the inelegant but forceful comment of a delegate at last year's SNP conference.

Our country has been contaminated from the Borders to the Highlands. We carry the most powerful instruments of death in the world, ironically in the Holy Loch. We are resisting being forced to take the Trident missile and the Torness nuclear plant.

We're meeting again in the village hall. There will be another march, more speeches, I hope another ceilidh. But there will also be more anger. We want neither nuclear energy, waste nor

weapons. Look out for the Ullapool banner at the next London
demonstration.

*They invited grandmothers to one of their meetings at Faslane where
Kay stood and spoke what was more a prayer than a poem. When she
finished, one of the policewomen escorting the demonstration was
shedding tears.*

FASLANE: REMEMBER

We remember our lives
We remember.
We remember our sisters
We remember
We remember our grandmothers
We remember our mothers
We remember the womb that bore us.
We remember the joy and the pain
We remember becoming women
We remember the hot flow of blood
We remember the loss of virginity
We remember the joy and the pain
We remember the child in our womb
We remember the breaking of the waters
We remember the pain and the joy
We remember the children growing
We remember the stopping of the flow
We remember the promise of another birth
We remember our child's child
We remember our awe at the miracle
We remember our passionate love

We remember our sisters in other countries
We remember the grandmothers of Russia and America
We remember the grandmothers of Europe, Asia and
Africa
We remember the grandmothers of Israel and the
Lebanon
We remember the grandmothers of China
We remember the grandmothers of Japan
We remember the grandmothers of the Philippines and
Nicaragua
We remember the grandmothers of South Africa
We remember the grandmothers who have been tortured
We remember the grandmothers who have been raped
We remember the grandmothers who have been
imprisoned.
We remember all the grandmothers who have suffered in
the cause of peace and justice
We remember our own experience of war
We remember the sound of tears.

Saints & Sinners, New Society, Vol. 66, November 17ᵗʰ 1983, p. 295

If there is any truth in reincarnation theory, I must have been a hoofed creature in a previous existence. I am absolutely terrified of cattle grids. In spite of that, an hour before dawn one morning last week, I crossed one of these gruesome obstacles in an unsuccessful and illicit attempt to enter a NATO base.

The intention was quite harmless – to plant a Peace rosebush and some bulbs in ground, currently said to cover 20,000 tons of weapons, and to claim my right to walk on land that has been taken out of common use. With some friends from Glasgow's Centrepeace and the Faslane peace camp, I was trying to find a way in.

We scrambled across heather, bog, fallen trees, two railway lines and a barbed wire fence just slightly higher than my legs are long. All this in the dark. As we dodged, stumbled, crawled on our bellies to avoid lights and guards, I was overtaken, as so often, by a sense of the glorious absurdity of human behaviour. But I could also taste the excitement, the drama and a sense of significant action so rarely found in our daily lives.

Reaching the perimeter fence we lay watching the Ministry of Defence police below us in the valley. We had spent the previous night in our little tented village at the main gate of the base, listening to their dogs howl and their cars patrol up and down the boundaries. Glen Douglas, where the weapons are buried, is one of the many magnificent glens in Strathclyde. The whole area bristles with weapons – Faslane, Coulport, the Holy Loch, are all within a 29-mile radius, and Trident is to be added.

My sense of impotence about all of that was reinforced by the height of the fence, strung 10-feet high between concrete posts and crowned by barbed wire. There was no way I could climb it, but three of my companions did with the help of the rest of us. They had no way back, except under police escort through the gate. But the rose bush was planted to the sound of the alarm whistle.

The rest of us plodded back, the sense of absurdity past, grateful that a few people had for a moment reclaimed the land for a wholesome use.

Later in the day, I sat with a friend in the sun, cheerfully singing metric psalms, and realised that

'I to the hills will lift mine eyes,

from whence doth come mine aid' has been given a new meaning in the Scottish hills.

Saints & Sinners, New Society, Vol. 68, May 3rd 1984, p.199

Twenty-three years ago I took my daughter on the first CND march from Dunoon to the Holy Loch. This year I took my four-year-old granddaughter. She was wearing a badge saying, 'I want to grow up, not blow up.'

I once heard Isaiah Berlin say that any institution that fails to achieve its goals in 25 years never will. He reasoned that in that time it puts down roots in the established order, which make it impossible to truly challenge it. Is CND becoming the respectable ritualised opposition which makes us all feel less guilty, more comfortable, less compelled to take any personal responsibility for nuclear weapons in Britain?

Certainly our Easter demonstration was ritualised. We paraded neatly, marched tidily, made very little noise, did what the police told us. We listened to speeches and sang a few nostalgic songs in an orderly and – if truth be told – rather desultory way. Many seemed to be there from a sense of duty rather than conviction.

Three days later I went to Dunoon Sheriff Court to hear two Greenham women being tried for offences they were alleged to have committed last January when they had come up to support a Women for Peace demonstration at the American base. I remembered that day well. It was freezing cold; the snow was thick on the ground. I had returned from sweltering Bangkok the day before. In spite of that it was a joyful and creative experience.

Three months later they brought the same spirit to the bleak, vaulted, woodlined courtroom. The women and their three friends lit the place up like birds of paradise with their gay clothes, their odd hairstyles, their vivid personalities. They both pleaded not guilty but an irascible sheriff was unimpressed by what they had to say. He imposed swingeing fines. I was left with no sense that justice had been done.

One of them, a beautiful strong seventeen-year-old, charged with malicious damage, took over her own defence. She had, in fact, sprayed the women's symbol on the American cinema wall... Already a rather grubby wall. She said, 'It was not sprayed, as I have been charged, 'maliciously'. It was sprayed in defiance, in strength, because of my love of life and of the earth. I contend that I have committed no crime – the malice lies within the walls of the base...'

I hope that if my granddaughter gets the chance to grow up, and not blow up, she too will love life as much.

Saints & Sinners, New Society, Vol 74. November 22nd 1985, p.330

Taking part in an action at Faslane and living permanently in the peace camp on the roadside near the submarine base are two very different things. The first requires commitment and the capacity to take risks – particularly for women, after reported strip searches in a Glasgow police station. But it also offers drama, comradeship and an audience. It takes a different sort of courage to stay after the demonstrators' cars have driven off and the excitement has died down.

There are about 20 men and women in the camp now, facing the winter in a collection of caravans and huts which will soon become too cold to sit around in during the day and too expensive to heat individually. They will therefore be forced to share one large one for eating, reading, talking, mending and all the other things one does between breakfast and supper. 'Like living in a submarine', one said.

You might only have interests in common with two or three others, but you've got to be able to get on with everyone because, besides demonstrating against the base, you are trying to apply in your own life the principles of the peace movement. And 'everyone' might include anyone. In a world short of sanctuaries for vulnerable or disturbed people, the camp draws some who are looking for help to sort out their own lives rather than the nuclear problem.

The confidence of damaged people begins to flower in this accepting environment, where you're not having to prove yourself all the time. Some come wreathed in cynicism, believing everyone and everything in the world to be bad and nuclear annihilation inevitable. In spite of the constant pressure of the base, they usually change too as optimism re-emerges.

As each becomes stronger, they can in turn offer help to others. Everyone agrees that talking is the great medium of help, but doesn't always work. After weeks of agonising, a few have been asked to leave. This leaves a massive sense of failure, but because camp life and hassles with the police are so testing, there is a level of personal stability without which people grow worse, not better, if they stay.

Local residents are often hostile. *They're* not worried about the bomb, they say. But after a recent earth tremor in Argyll, the police phones were jammed with frightened inquiries about the missiles. The camp is changing its nature, settling down for the long haul and sending out roots into other community organisations. 'Not as exciting' they say ruefully, 'as going out in the night and cutting the fence'.

They haven't stopped doing that, I'm glad to say, because their strength lies in bringing the horror of the base down to a dimension that can be attacked by human beings. 'We can walk up to the gate with our rainbow banners and not feel helpless,' is how they put it

In another of her columns Kay reflected sharply on the attitude of the established church to nuclear weapons.

By coincidence, I was driving along Holy Loch while listening to the Church of England debate on nuclear weapons. From the radio I could hear the measured, received pronunciation of the Archbishop of Canterbury saying that to disarm unilaterally would have little effect. Beside me on the loch, I could see the Polaris 'mother' ship, as it is obscenely called, with the small grey submarine which carries the warheads tucked in at its side.

I don't know how the world was created. But that day it was fantastically beautiful. Snow on the hills, blue sky, blue water. The sun made everything sparkle and glitter. I tried to imagine what it might be like inside that London hall where the aristocracy of the church was meeting.

They call themselves Christians, but it was hard to find any common theme, other than that they all referred familiarly to God, assuring each other that He was concerned with peace... Even the Chaplain to the fleet was sure about that.

What I have never understood, if that is true, is why so many Christian churches decorate their walls with military flags and regimental colours. They seem to me to pollute a space that has as its primary purpose the worship of the Creator, rather than destruction. Whether you believe in no god, an Old Testament god or the god of Jesus, such barbaric tribal practices arouse incredulity. And how can priests and ministers become chaplains, serving both Christ and a war machine?

I didn't doubt the sincerity of anyone who spoke in the debate. But I believe increasingly that sincerity is one of the cheapest human emotions. Each of us sincerely clings to our prejudices. Hitler is one of the most sincere figures in history.

The Bishop of Birmingham's speech was for me the most helpful. He explained what I hadn't previously understood. The New Testament, he averred, has no teaching to offer in the nuclear debate. It deals exclusively with the ethics of personal behaviour. Jesus, it seems, gave no teaching on the morality of the state.... The ethics of personal behaviour bear no relationship to that. You cannot expect a nation to turn the other cheek. Within that view, I suppose, war banners in churches and chaplains are quite logical.

In spite of the odd flash of religious feeling from a man like Paul Oestreicher it was a very secular debate. He proposed 'a holy foolishness... And unilateral disarmament.' Few women's voices were heard. The quality of thought overall was poorer than in the average political party conference, although the accents were posher than in any of them. If people build gods in their own image, then the majority god of the Church of England clergy who voted against unilateralism is not very attractive... Or very holy. I've always thought it ironic that these evil weapons should be based on the Holy Loch.

The 'Horts' – the women in Kay's peace group – would not have been satisfied if they had only participated in orderly demonstrations. One by one they engaged in acts that led to prison sentences, and Kay soon felt her turn was due. She wrote about the experience in an article for the Glasgow Herald, entitled 'Prison system 'designed to degrade'~', published on July 4th, 1986.

Cornton Vale

A few weeks ago the Glasgow Herald sent me a review copy of a book called 'The Imprisonment of Woman'. It tells the story of the treatment of women in prison and describes the present regime in Cornton Vale, Scotland's only prison for women. When I was reading it I was not aware that I would soon be having a personal experience of what its authors describe.

On June 30th, in the morning, I appeared before Sheriff Murphy at Dumbarton Sheriff Court on a charge that I did 'without reasonable excuse, wilfully or recklessly damage property, namely, a section of wire perimeter fence belonging to another and did cut said wire or perimeter fence; contrary to the Criminal Justice (Scotland) Act 1980, Section 78 (1).'

To be explicit, I had cut one strand in the fence round the submarine base at Faslane as a symbolic gesture against the evil weapons being stored there and the preparations being carried out for new Trident weapons. I was one of a group of eighteen protesting in this way after notifying the police and public that we intended to take this action.

I defended myself and was courteously and scrupulously guided through the correct procedures by Sheriff Murphy. Appearing as an alleged law breaker is not an easy experience for any of us, but being granted personal dignity, as I think Sheriff Murphy does for all who come into his court, goes a long way to reinforcing what respect we may have for its processes.

I was arguing that I had very 'reasonable excuse' for demonstrating in the way I had done – namely that since the Nuremberg trials which had condemned Nazis as war criminals for going along with the evil policies of their government without protest, I had a duty in conscience to protest if my own government were making plans to carry out the evil act of destroying cities with weapons 2000 times more powerful than the bomb which was dropped on Hiroshima.

The sheriff didn't agree with my interpretation, sentenced me to a fine of £70 – £50 and £20 costs for my share of replacing the fence – and I refused to pay. I was then sentenced to fourteen days in prison and taken downstairs by a woman police officer to a cell, which I shared with a distressed young woman still awaiting trial. She was the first of many sisters in the spirit to whose pain I was to be exposed in the next few days.

Before long I was taken (*in a bus collecting women from courts across the West of Scotland*) to the women's cells in the new District Court in Glasgow. Built underground, modern, hygienic, they are given warmth and humanity by the turnkey, Susan (I don't know her second name, we had met before and she called me Kay) who gives food and loving care to everyone who needs it, and that was most of us.

All my possessions had been taken away from me but I could see a clock, which helped me to keep in touch with reality. It was the last I was to see for some time. At 5.30pm, thirteen of us, some first offenders, some experienced, some shaky with the after effects of a drinking binge, all of us under stress, were handcuffed together and taken in a large bus to Cornton Vale.

Driving past, no one would think it was a prison. It was designed to merge into the landscape and consists of long low blocks set in very attractive gardens. We were taken into a reception area, released from the handcuffs, and stood in a queue to have our 'particulars' taken. After this each of us was sent to a small cubicle, told to undress then go to the shower and use a delousing shampoo.

We were then given prison clothes of reasonable quality – two simple heavy cotton dresses, a nightdress and dressing gown, slippers, a cardigan, an anorak and heavy shoes. I had taken underwear with me in case I was sentenced and I was allowed to keep this. The whole procedure was carried out pleasantly and efficiently with the help of prisoners as aides to the officers.

The first lesson I had to learn was that every opportunity for making choices of any kind had been stripped away from me. If I did exactly what I was told I would have no problems, but I had ceased to be a person who could make any decisions. My cooperation was not sought, only my obedience or conformity. For me the most offensive demonstration of this was that I was not asked by what name I wished to be called. From the beginning I was called Catherine – the name on my court order – and under the rules prisoners are instructed to call the officers 'Miss'. The governor and assistant governors (all men) have to be called 'Sir'.

I was too emotionally drained on the first night to cope with confrontation but after being taken across to the block where I was expecting to live for the next ten days, being locked in to the pleasant small room that every prisoner has, and getting a night's sleep, I realised I must express my objections to this practice.

It seemed to me to sum up the power the staff wield over prisoners. It throws a mask of caring over the relationship, but denies equality. It also carries powerful messages of social class. Some women call their daily helps by their first names but do not expect their own first names to be used. I made it clear that I was perfectly happy to have my first name used if I in turn could call staff by their first names. Equally, if they called me 'Mrs.' or 'Ms.' Carmichael I would happily call them by their formal names. Both ideas were rejected with horror.

Most of the staff found my attitude difficult to understand or accept, seeing it as threatening to authority and their own status. But the women with whom I was imprisoned had no difficulty, except for those who had been successfully conditioned over the years to accept their social inferiority. What many found particularly hard was having to call an officer, perhaps years younger than themselves, 'Miss'. They found this degrading and humiliating. We, of course, called each other by our first names and I was enormously grateful for the loving support and help they gave me.

The pattern of the day is very strictly organised. Each prisoner lives in a unit of seven rooms along a corridor, which leads to two lavatories, a shower, a bath, a kitchen and a sitting room where meals are eaten. There is also a small office for staff. The physical conditions are very good and bear no comparison with conditions for men prisoners. We were wakened at 6 am to wash, dress and strip beds before making breakfast.

After eating (with plastic cutlery and using plastic cups of which there were always too few to go round) we had to collect cleaning materials and clean the whole unit. Every bit of the floor was brushed then washed by hand every day. As a result of an accident the previous week my right hand was covered by a plaster so I asked for a rubber glove to protect the broken skin. The staff were very helpful and scoured the institution – regretfully being able to produce only two left hand gloves, both of which turned out to have holes in them.

I cheerfully washed floors, being grateful for the exercise, since formal opportunities are limited to 20 minutes a day, but could not help wondering why in 1986 it was considered necessary to do that by hand rather than by using a squeezie mop which is what most people do in their homes.

The rest of the days were a blur of being locked up, staff shouting at prisoners, being taken to the work-room, being taken back for lunch and the 20-minute exercise which consisted of walking round in a circle like something out of an American movie, being locked up again, going back to work, being brought back for the last meal of the day at 4.30 pm, being locked in once more until 6 pm, then allowed to shower, wash one's dress or iron, then compulsory 'association' (which means watching TV until 8) having tea and toast and then being locked into one's room until next morning.

Since no clock was ever on view and the time could only be discovered by asking an officer, the whole experience was highly disorienting. It was another small demonstration of power being taken away, but this was only one example of a multiplicity of minor humiliations, some of which were deliberately inflicted by officers who chose to use their power in petty ways, along with others which even the officers who were genuinely trying to be civilised were causing.

It is the system itself that is designed to degrade, using techniques which are redolent of the Poor Law. It forced me to consider the possible advantages of privatisation.

Being a protester for peace means that I feel I have to work at creating peaceful and creative relations within my own life and with other human beings. I do not find that easy, particularly when I encounter people who use their authority to attack human dignity either in myself or in others. I recognise that they do this in order to compensate for their own feelings of inadequacy and I try to understand that and forgive them.

To do that I have to seek something in them that I can love. But equally I want to stop them using people whom they have in their power to feed their egos. That can only be done by changing prison policies and routines, by appropriate selection and training of staff, and by clear statements of the values all staff are expected to uphold.

There are far more women in prison in Scotland than need to be there. I argued when Cornton Vale was being built to hold more than 200 women that it was not required. There cannot be more than 20 women in Scotland who need secure containment, if even that number. They could be housed more sanely and far more cheaply in a small, secure group of bungalows.

What we need is more accommodation in the community for elderly women – who may have a drink problem – to which they can be taken if they assault our policemen; treatment facilities for women with problems of addiction; more sophisticated services for women who may not quite fit the categories of mental illness defined as suitable for admission to mental hospitals; and better community support services for women who fiddle social security or steal from supermarkets – plus a variety of alternative tasks and penalties to be worked through while living in the community.

I have not written about the pain and distress endured by the women whom I met in prison. Separated from their families, particularly their children, many of them had cried themselves to exhaustion night after night. I can't write about that because the experience of encountering that grief is still too raw for me. I used to see the struggle for world peace as a separate issue from questions of human justice, but I no longer see that as a tenable distinction. They have to be thought of together as peace and justice.

Injustice precludes peace though it may compel docility. Every woman can see something of her own life in every woman in Cornton Vale. We are all sisters joined in our capacity to love and to bleed. I wish every woman could have the opportunity to experience as I did a few days of life as a prisoner.

Certainly everyone should read the book *The Imprisonment of Woman*, (by *Dobash, Dobash and Gutteridge*), which tells in more detail than I can give here the facts about a system which in physical conditions is better than it used to be when it was housed in an old jail building, but which has tightened the net of submission, powerlessness, sexism and humiliation around everyone who enters.

Kay was writing a book review and a valuable essay on an important field of social policy, so she omitted much that she told me on her return from prison – some of which should not be lost.

On her first morning, prison officers refused to accept the offer she made to answer to her first name if they would allow her to address them by theirs. 'No. You call us Ma'am,' she was told. So she said that in that case she would not respond to them, and was sent on a charge of insubordination to the Governor of the jail. (A man – in Scotland's only prison for women.) After an interview, which was unproductive for both of them, she was sent back to her corridor, given a bucket and brush and ordered to scrub the floor outside the door of her room. To show there was no ill feeling she scrubbed and wiped down the whole corridor – with her one usable hand and arm.

Meanwhile, bouquets of flowers began to arrive, sent by friends who had heard she was in prison. The first was thrust into a bucket and dumped on the floor of her cell. As more and more were delivered, she asked that they be given to women in neighbouring cells and, before long, all of them had flowers.

Later in the day she put in a request to talk with the officer in charge of her corridor. Called eventually into the office where there were several of them, the senior one asked what she wanted. 'I want to speak to the Chaplain,' she said. 'But you told us you have no religion'. 'That's right,' said Kay. 'But I have a spiritual problem'. 'And what is your spiritual problem?' she was asked, in a voice heavy with sarcasm. 'I am finding it very difficult to love the Governor'. As they struggled to contain their laughter it became obvious that they all had much the same problem.

'Very well. Do you want to see the Minister or the Priest?'

'Both' said Kay.

But before those meetings could take place, a lady arrived at the prison gates and paid her fine. Kay was promptly given her possessions and discharged into a wet, dark evening, wondering how she could get to Stirling station and a train to Glasgow. A car drove out towards her. It was the prison social worker, going home late, who stopped and gave her a lift. She had been one of Kay's students.

Next day she sent, anonymously, a large bouquet of flowers to the prison officers.

Kay was disappointed not to have served her full sentence and never discovered who had paid her fine. I have since learned it was Helen Liddle (whom she described in one of her articles as 'The best Secretary of State Scotland ever had'). Joe Haines (the Prime Minister's Press Secretary) and possibly other friends from her time working at No. 10 Downing Street also played a part in this kind, if unwanted, act of generosity.

Saints & Sinners, 4.10.85, p.32

About an anti-nuclear vigil in Glasgow and why they did these things.

Six o'clock, on a damp Friday night in Glasgow, at the junction of Buchanan Street and Argyll Street, in a cold wind is not the most exciting place in the world. But it has begun to develop a certain style since it has become the site of the vigil against Trident campaign.

For example, our home-made banner is handsomely colourful. Today we have solemn exhibitions in museums of the great banners of the early trade union movement. If we survive (and it is towards that end we're vigiling), this one will be worthy of a place in an exhibition of peace movement banners. Some of us who turn up are pretty stylish too in our fashionable multi-layered clothes… or was that last season's look? But the most colourful people are our visitors.

One of them wandered over and, breathing alcohol fumes, inquired our intentions with genuine interest. He was an immediate sympathiser. Some 20 years ago he had demonstrated in O'Connell Street for peace between the Catholics and Protestants in Northern Ireland and had been picked up by the police as a result and charged with breach of the peace. This had seemed very unfair to him.

He had since gone down in the world but retained his belief in peace and freedom, despite recurrent encounters with policemen and jailers. On his first appearance at Bow Street he had been offered £30 or thirty days. He had said to the magistrate, 'I'll take the £30 your Honour. Thank you very much,' and had been done for contempt of court, ending up in Pentonville.

He generously offered us all a drink from his bottle to keep the cold out, but agreed that it wouldn't do our cause any good to be seen slugging back the whisky. He then left, wishing us luck, to spend the night on a bench somewhere, still cheerful, not yet at the end of his capacities but working hard at getting there.

Some of the others were disparaging, asking what good it would all do? How can one explain that we were there as much for the good of our own souls as trying to influence decisions about Trident – to recall once a week for an hour some of the horrifying realities of our time and to reflect on them.

A passer-by, who had been a teenage Aldermarston marcher in the sixties, got the point and walked thoughtfully away. At seven o'clock we self-consciously sang a peace roundel and left. But we'll be back next Friday from six o'clock till seven. If you're in the area, do pay us a visit.

V

LILYBANK

When Kay was Deputy Chair of the Supplementary Benefits Commission, which had a general responsibility for the means-tested social security benefits on which our poorest people depend, she felt she should gain some experience of the lives they lead, the income they had to survive on, and the community in which she might herself have been living if she had not escaped from her childhood home. In this article she wrote about the first days of this experience.

In the spring of 1976 I was given permission by the University of Glasgow to have a period of study leave. This is a civilised arrangement by which University teachers and others are given paid leave to pursue private interests that will improve their ability to do their job. Arrangements like this are particularly important in the teaching of subjects that are concerned with people's lives like social work and social administration. It is very easy to become involved in academic theories of how people behave and to stop seeing the people. This is particularly liable to happen when the teaching of students is concerned with the provision of services to that section of our community whom we call poor or disadvantaged, since neither the teachers nor the students are likely to number poor or disadvantaged people among their friends and neighbours.

A very few students may come from areas which are considered disadvantaged, but simply by being University students will be cut off emotionally and it is very unlikely that they will continue to live in those areas after qualifying. No University teachers are likely to be found living in areas of acute social disadvantage. Some of us try to maintain an opportunity to practice social work to keep what skills we acquired in our training alive, but also because we believe that while practice without theory may be blind, theory without practice can be very sterile. It is not easy to find opportunities to do this in the part-time way necessary when combining it with academic teaching, but for those of us who do it is very rewarding. I myself have kept in touch through work in prisons and borstals. I chose this because it seemed to me that these institutions constantly confront us with the failure of our society to deal with basic problems of employment, education and housing. Our prisons are dustbins for the poor and disadvantaged. They are the ultimate in policies of exclusion.

There is at the end of the day always something artificial in taking the professional role of the social worker, or for that matter, the doctor, the teacher, or social security officer... They need another person to turn them into a professional...They have to give a name to that other person... So they call him a client, a patient, a pupil or a claimant, and by doing that too often deny his existence as a person. Like actors in a play, each learns from experience what is expected of them and when they meet they are ready to read from pre-prepared scripts...

I realised, with a sinking heart, that there was no way I could avoid the logic of my thinking. I was being relentlessly pushed to finding a way of dipping myself back into the water of poverty and I had no alternative but to do it in my own city. The task to be faced was the one that lay under my hand, no matter how unpromising since it was the only one I could do and I had to do it as well as I could. These decisions were not clearly thought out. I was being influenced more by my inner life of feeling than by my processes of rational thought and decided to go along with that part of myself and see what happened. I wrote to the Director of Housing asking to rent a local authority house (in Scotland flats are called houses) for a period of three months starting on October 1st. This I thought would take me up to Christmas. I said that I wanted it as a base for a research study concerned with the socialisation of children. I had decided that the most important aim for me would be to look at the way children lived and developed in an area of deprivation. I made no qualification as to where I should go except that it should be in the East End, in a disadvantaged area and that there should be lots of children.

I then had to apply myself to the question of how I would present myself to the community. If I moved into a deprived area wearing my normal mask I would be identified as a social worker and inevitably pushed into the role of being a 'helping' person. I wanted to become part of the community and realised that I would have to modify my appearance. Going to 'the Barrows' in the East End, a large market area open on Saturdays and Sundays, I looked at obviously disadvantaged women of about my own age to see what was different between me and them. This could be analysed quite easily. It consisted of: hairstyle, make-up, clothes and accessories, speech, ways of holding your body, and shoes. *She acquired a complete set of clothes.* The total cost of these purchases was £15.10.

I had to make a decision about money. How much was I going to allow myself? I decided that I would live on the amount that would have been available had I been a social security claimant, and what help I would have got if I had been moving without resources into local authority housing. *Consulting the regional social security office about exceptional needs payments that would be made to a single woman discharged from mental hospital or leaving a broken marriage, she learnt what she could spend in second-hand shops on furniture and household equipment.*

Next came a telephone call telling me to pick up the keys of 90 Dunning Street, 2 up right, in the Lilybank Scheme. It was only about a mile away from Shettleston Road where I had lived as a child and practically next door to Tollcross Park where I had played *(and educated herself in the public library between the ages of seven and ten.)*

I picked up the keys from the factor's office. While waiting in the inevitable queue an elderly lady came up to me waving a form and asked me if I knew what she was supposed to do. There were different forms for different types of repair: glazing, plumbing, joinery. She wanted a plumbing form for a lavatory repair but there were none available. I suggested we score out the trade on the form she was holding and write in the word 'plumber'. She was nervous about doing such an anarchistic act but ultimately agreed. She thanked me, then said 'You'll be a school teacher hen?'

The factor's office was unbelievably dreary, with one chair only. Enquiries were dealt with at a small window, which required all except the smallest person to stoop in order to present their face to the clerk on the other side. I was given the lease to sign, handed the keys, told what dates to pay my rent and went on my way. *She then went to a furniture shop near the Barrows and got a single bed and a pillow for £36.50.*

But how to cut off my retreat? Some friends of mine were in need of temporary accommodation in Glasgow so I offered them my home. This meant I would not go back even for the odd night or weekend. I resigned temporarily from the Supplementary Benefits Commission. The only person there to whom I told my real intention was my Chairman, David Donnison. He was the only person who gave me immediate support in my venture. Everyone else thought I was being distinctly eccentric.

I was engaging in a purely private exercise with no goals other than to improve my own awareness. For this reason I decided to use the name of the grandmother with whom I had lived in Shettleston Road and after whom I was named Catherine Price – *which became the name she adopted for the next three months.*

Kay consulted a colleague with many years experience of anthropological fieldwork about her project but he only said 'just go ahead and do it'. Then, after clearing up her office, preparing her home for the friends who were borrowing it and arranging for her mail to be redirected to her daughter Sheena, she drove out to see the street she would be going to. It looked desolate. I drove through Dunning Street, quickly craning my neck to look up at the windows of 2 up right at number 90. To my dismay they looked broken and I drove away quickly, wondering what I had let myself in for.

I found out the next morning.

I had ordered a taxi and left with a suitcase containing my clothes, a radio, a tape recorder, four books and a sleeping bag, a hammer, a screw driver and some nails and a ball of string – my survival kit – *grabbing a sweeping brush as she left the house.* Dressed for the first time in my new clothes, wearing no make-up and with a headscarf on, I looked at myself in the mirror, then put on a pair of national health service spectacles. I left Kay Carmichael behind and went out as Mrs. Price.

Arriving in Dunning Street, I am used to taxi drivers in Glasgow being helpful to me, coming round if you are carrying bags and helping you out. This driver simply sat there and let me struggle out, the first of a number of differences I began to notice...

Kay struggled up the two flights of stairs with her suitcase and brush and entered her new home. There she found a newly modernised kitchen and one room in which she could place the newly delivered bed. But the two rooms on the other side of the house, facing the street, were indescribable. Every window was broken and the floor was covered with broken glass and stones. The bathroom had one broken window and the bath was full of its fragments, but the bath, wash hand basin and lavatory pan were new. I had been allocated one of the newly modernised houses I had been reading about. *She set about sweeping up the mess.*

There was a gas stove, but neither it nor anything electrical would work. After fruitlessly trying all the switches she found a kind neighbour who told her where to seek help at the 'modernisation office' – fortunately in the same street. It was locked, although the notice on the door said it should have been open... the first of many similar experiences. Kafka used to write about his feelings when this kind of thing happened. I wouldn't be surprised if he was a council tenant at some time in his life. I moved on to the factor's office to report my broken windows, convinced that there had been a minor oversight in allowing me to move into a house in this condition. I had to walk about a mile to the factor's office. There was no bus route but it was a cheerful autumn day and I enjoy walking. It did occur to me that if it had been raining and I had also to cope with a couple of children under five I might feel differently about it. I was really seeing the scheme for the first time and its ugliness hit me like a blow. The streets were littered with rubbish and there seemed to be waste ground on two sides. I cut across and made my way in the general direction of Parkhead Cross.

Parkhead huddles round its Cross, dereliction all round it where its slum buildings have been pulled down. It had been an important place in my childhood and adolescence. It had ladies and gents outfitters where I was taken to buy major new items of clothing. Part of the ritual of my life had been that every Easter Sunday everyone should go to Mass dressed in new clothes. Ideally this meant everything from the skin out, including new shoes. Every effort was made to arrange this for children but for adults it was clearly not possible. What was done was that at least one new item should be seen to be worn, a hat or gloves – something. For years all my Easter clothes were bought at Campbell's. I could remember the smell of it, the orderliness, the supercilious sales ladies, the racks of clothes, the polished brown linoleum and the magical wires far above my head that carried the money from the counter to the cash desk. All that was left of that magnificent establishment was one small shop of ladies' and children's wear. The rest of the building was taken over by a motley collection of shops selling toys, furniture, televisions, and a bank.

The other powerful memory I had of Parkhead Cross was as a great centre of political meetings. There had been a remarkable member of Parliament called John McGovern who had represented the Shettleston Constituency (which included Parkhead) for the Independent Labour Party, which was the great radical party founded by Keir Hardie. It had split away from the Labour Party and pursued more left-wing and pacifist policies. McGovern had been a great thorn in the side of the orthodox Labour Party, particularly during the war years. He was a witty, mischievous speaker who revelled in a rough house. I had been evacuated to the countryside during the war and returned a committed socialist and pacifist. The only choices open to an East End youngster were the Communist Party and the Independent Labour Party. The Labour Party at that time did not count in Glasgow. My pacifism eliminated the Communist Party *(who believed the working class should prepare for the revolution by learning to use arms)* and I joined the Independent Labour Party. Among other great experiences this meant that I became involved in the rough and tumble of public meetings at places like Parkhead Cross. That morning, walking past the corner of the Cross, I could still see him standing, a stocky charismatic figure dominating a crowd of about two hundred people without even the benefit of a microphone. The Independent Labour Party specialised in charismatic figures. I later came to realise that McGovern was essentially a clever, lovable rascal and this was illustrated at his funeral where to be on the safe side he was ushered off by a Requiem Mass from the Roman Catholic Church, an oration by Moral Re-armament and a secular service. He needed no other memorial – that said it all.

By the time I got to the factor's office I had almost forgotten why I was there but the depressing surroundings reminded me of my broken windows. I remembered the lady I had met on my last visit so I looked first for the appropriate form to request a visit for a glazier. There wasn't one, so I adopted the principle I had advised and firmly scored out 'PLASTERER' and substituted 'GLAZIER'. I then filled in the form and joined the queue only to be told that all notices for repair had to be pushed through a letter box set into the wall beside the enquiry desk. I had decided that under no circumstances was I going to try to get any special consideration. I was simply going to go through the same motions as any other tenant. I knew I possessed what are called middle class skills. I knew how to make a fuss and get things done. Normally there would have been no question of me going physically to a factor's office – I would have telephoned – but for the first time for many years I had no telephone in my house. It was therefore with some uncertainty that I pushed my form through the anonymous letterbox and set off to find a bus to take me to the Electricity Office and the Gas Board Office. The district I was seeking for my electricity was Dennistoun. Just as Parkhead was up market from Lilybank so Dennistoun is up market from Parkhead, with better quality shops, better dressed people and more shoppers with motorcars. It lies about two miles from Parkhead. The fare was nine pence – and I suddenly realised I was going to have to watch things like bus fares. The electricity lady was helpful and promised that someone would call that afternoon. At the Gas Board Office the gasman was cheerful but unhelpful and said the gas is never cut off so the fault must lie somewhere else. I walked another mile to Woolworths and bought a downie, curtains, a shovel, a pail, a scrubbing brush and soap, at a total cost of £17.80. By this time I was harassed and exhausted and it was beginning to show. The kindness of the ladies working in the store overwhelmed me. As a result of having polio as a child I can only properly use one of my arms. Woolworths is not known for the effectiveness of its paper bags but these ladies wrapped everything securely for me in brown paper and I staggered out of the shop, thought about the other mile I would need to walk to the bus stop, rejected the idea and hailed a taxi, deciding to deduct the fare from my fictional exceptional needs payment.

By this time my neighbour, Mrs. V, had arrived home from her part-time job, heard about me from her husband and kindly invited me in for a cup of tea. I now confronted the first of many differences in the way I live and the way other people live. For many years I have not drunk tea or coffee. This was clearly very eccentric in a community where having a cup of tea is much more significant than the simple act. It symbolises giving, receiving, kindness, hospitality. But Mrs. V coped marvellously with my deviance and produced Bovril plus a sliced sausage sandwich – more memories of childhood. Their house was extremely comfortable, furnished to a very high standard. They told me the story of the modernisation process, which was still going on in the rest of the Scheme, although this block was now finished. Tenants had a choice of being decanted to temporary accommodation or staying in the house and allowing the work to go on around them. Modernisation consisted of the installation of gas or electric central heating, a new kitchen with stainless steel sink and cupboard units, a new bathroom suite, a complete electrical rewiring with five electric points in the living room and one in each bedroom, a wardrobe built into one of the bedrooms, cracked ceilings renewed and papered, faulty door handles replaced, a new front door with electric bell and a new doorstep. The close and stairwells had been plastered and painted, the stairs surfaced with some kind of composition, the edges being protected with a brass rod sunk in, and window frames were replaced or mended and painted. The stonework on the outside of the building had also been cleaned. The Vs had chosen to stay in order to see that the work was properly carried out and described how awful it had been camping in one room with calor gas heater and cooker and with dirt and rubbish around them. But it had been, they felt, well worth it. Each tenant was given a money grant to have the house re-papered and painted. Old people or single parent families could have it done for them. If you took the grant, the house would be inspected within a year to make sure you had spent the money for its intended purpose and not on riotous living.

After caring for me, the Vs agreed to watch out for the electricity man while I had another attempt at the factor's office in Dunning Street. This time there was someone there. The door was opened for me by a young woman – obviously a local resident. I went in to find a young man, obviously on the defensive, surrounded by women who appeared to have taken over the flat. I realised later that this was not really the case, but it was as much as I could do at this stage to get him to listen to the story of my fire and say he would do something about it. I was left with the feeling that he saw my problem as very minor. I overcame the temptation to comment on the high temperature and comfort of the office and ask if I could spend the night there. I was finding uncomfortably aggressive thoughts beginning to dominate my mind. Back at the flat, my neighbours' son, who was visiting them, came up to see if he could light the fire – with no success. The fire was beginning to assume albatross proportions. I put up my new curtains by driving in some nails to hold the piece of string onto which I threaded the curtain. I wouldn't have had the ability or the energy to think of a curtain rail. I began to understand why poor people's curtains always look so slovenly. Balanced precariously on my neighbours' stepladder, haul though I might at the piece of string, I couldn't get it straight enough not to sag in the middle. Ultimately I drove in more nails and hitched the curtain up over them. I now felt slightly more civilised. I had a bed, a pillow, a sleeping bag, a downie and curtains up. To the critical observer it might not have seemed much but for me, bare boards and all, it had suddenly become home. So I next applied myself to what for the next week was going to be my constant spare time activity, pulling strips of loose, hanging paper off the walls.

In the end I spent the night without heat or light. No saviour came, no gasman, no electrician. I went to bed when it was getting dark and lay awake wondering what I was playing at. At my age surely I should have more sense than to be lying in a strange, cold, dark and empty house when I had a good comfortable home. That was the point when I realised how wise I had been to lend my house to my friends – otherwise I would have been up and away. I lay and let myself experience what I was feeling. To my surprise I realised I was afraid. I could hear people running up and down the stairs. I had worked in enough districts like this to know the potential violence in such communities and I remembered the frail lock on the front door. I tried to examine what I was afraid of – I had certainly nothing worth stealing and in any case no one would even know that the house was occupied with the front windows so blatantly broken. I decided I was simply afraid of the unknown and wondered, as I was so often to wonder, what it would have been like for someone really trying to make a new life for themselves outside a mental hospital, a broken marriage or a prison. It can be said that everyone has family or friends to help out. That is simply not true. Many people have no family to support them and if you have been in a mental hospital for a long time you may have no friends in the community. The same applies to someone coming out of prison, and a bad marriage can be another kind of prison. Of course, there are 'official' friends, social workers, but as we all know they are busy people and aren't going to be around to hold your hand in the dark. Lying there in the dark I began to understand in a new way why a mental hospital patient might prefer to go back to the label of being sick rather than take on this kind of loneliness, or the prisoner might find it simpler to be 'bad', and a woman might go back to a husband who ill-treated her. I fell asleep to waken somewhere in the night to great banging. The wind had risen and was whipping through the bedroom's broken windows to make the door whose lock was broken bash back and forward on its hinges. I struggled out. The room was sufficiently lit by street lamps for me to find a piece of string, tie the door to another door and stop it banging. There is something safe and peaceful about the middle of the night and I quickly fell back to sleep.

Next morning I woke early feeling full of energy but knowing that the experiences of the night had left an invisible mark. Somewhere the image of my confidence had been eroded. I decided to walk round the Scheme, get my bearings and buy some food. I knew from my neighbours that it had been built just over forty years ago and fitting that into my existing knowledge of the history of Glasgow housing I realised that it must have been part of the inter-war slum clearance programme. It seemed to be made up of about 500 houses. I discovered later it had 534. It was bordered on two sides by wasteland, on the third by factory buildings and on the fourth by a mainline Glasgow to London road. Even with the sun shining everything looked unutterably dreary. Some of this was certainly due to the modernisation programme – windows boarded up, dumps for old house fittings in the street – but years of underlying decay and destructive social attitudes were obvious. The buildings due to be modernised were neglected and vandalised, decorated with slogans like FUCK THE POPE, REMEMBER 1690, but more worrying was the fact that the newly modernised sections were showing signs of returning to their former state. In my own close the brass rods set into the stair edge had been ripped out before the composition in which they were set had properly dried, presumably to be sold to the nearest scrap merchant. On one of the pieces of waste ground a building was being erected. For weeks I asked people in the Scheme what was being built. No one knew and guesses ranged from a nursery school to a community centre for old people. Certainly both were needed. The children were more visible but at all times of the day if you were to walk along the streets with your eyes up you could see, at windows, old person after old person behind curtains staring out at the world.

I found two shops in the scheme. Both seemed to cater only for Lilybank people. And there was one some distance away on the main road which had a wider range of customers and therefore a wider range of goods. I bought some fruit for my breakfast – as yet I had no cooking facilities – and went back to stripping walls, sweeping up glass and stones in the front room, and waiting for the electricity man. Frustration is gradually building up, so to break it I rush up to the modernisation office with a strongly worded note. It is open, but with a long queue, so I hand the note in. Feelings of helplessness are beginning to take over from the frustration. To get some control I begin to work out my budget. So far I find I have spent £83.00 and haven't very much to show for it. I will have to get my living room papered even if not painted and still need floor covering, a table, chair, light bulbs, cutlery and something to cook on. I think about getting a part-time job. The reality of my financial situation has hit me.

I have the great gift of being able to fall asleep when under stress and I did this now. I wakened at 3.30 and decided to try the modernisation office again to remind them of my plight. Came back and was standing looking through my broken windows when I saw a yellow electricity van. I rushed down the stairs. It was just moving off and I planted myself firmly in front of it so that to avoid running me down it had to stop. A little computer in the back of my head was coolly observing the competent Kay Carmichael cracking up. I presented myself to the two men in the van as a helpless desperate female, which indeed I was, and pleaded for help – no authority in the voice now. They were kind and incredibly I was grateful. One of the men came with me and said I needed a fuse in the close. He went off to 'borrow' one from another close, put it in, but there was still no electricity. He retired defeated. Whatever was wrong was beyond his competence. He was ashamed and I could have wept. I had sanctioned a fuse coming from someone else's close and I knew that even if it meant depriving someone else of electricity I wanted mine on. I was reaching primitive responses in myself that I had not known existed. I rushed back up to the modernisation office, my fourth visit, and this time I made a fuss. I stood over the young man until he made a 'phone call to a mysterious place where someone said they would try to get someone that afternoon. I walked back to the flat, pursued by feelings of helplessness, and shock at the speed with which I had become a victim. It seemed to me at that moment that if there was one thing I was able to do for this community it would be to attempt to restore trust in the simplest possible ways – like officials, tradesmen and professional people keeping their promises. I knew from stories I had heard from a wide range of the receivers of services that this was the greatest single source of irritation. I myself had been kept waiting only a few months earlier in the Outpatient Department of my local infirmary. Given a two o'clock appointment I left at 3.45 unseen by the consultant because I myself had been given an appointment for four o'clock which I was not prepared to break. People like my 'old' self had resources to combat the feelings of rage and helplessness this kind of situation arouses. We know how to complain, how to use the old boy and girl network, how to pay for private and privileged attention. Not so the tenants of Lilybank. For them every official has a monopoly of power, no fences bend for them, they are hemmed in.

I was still thinking these thoughts when the door was knocked and a plumber arrived. He was a beautifully competent man who quickly took the whole fire out to disclose behind it a supply tap that should have been turned on but wasn't. He said I should also have been given a small instruction sheet about how to light the pilot light in the fire, an operation that seemed to me to be extremely complicated and, in fact, was not possible for me using only one arm. I realised later that I should have asked him how the gas central heating worked. It was to remain forever a mystery for me along with everyone else in Lilybank to whom I spoke. Either they kept it on all the time and kept the windows open, or like me were so afraid of the cost they never turned the radiators on. My neighbours showed me how to heat the hot water.

My next visitor was the Master of Works, another competent man – the telephone call had obviously borne fruit. He said the electricity circuit had been broken and he would have it attended to. Fifteen minutes later I had both light and heat. My joy was unconfined. I felt like a baby discovering the world.

These were just the first two days of Kay's stay in Lilybank. There was much more to come. As no glazier came to repair her broken windows and darker, colder days drew on, she followed the example she observed

*among her neighbours. Spotting a man in overalls getting into a van –
symbols of power in this community – she ran down to ask him for help
in repairing her windows and patching up her walls: a situation he was
clearly accustomed to. He returned at the weekend and, with Council
tools and materials, did a good job. Asking what she owed him for this
revealed that he charged at three different rates. As a woman on her own
without a job she was given the lowest.*

*Once a fortnight Kay drew from her bank the sum she would have been
given had she been living on supplementary benefit. She found it difficult
to eat the awful and unhealthy food available in local shops. Jimmy Boyle,
who was the only person in Barlinnie Jail's Special Unit who knew where
she was, had guessed this would be a problem. He was writing regularly
to her, knew where she was living and the name she had adopted, so he
made an attractive salad for her and asked one of his visitors to take it
to her. (A small kindness, by the man often described as Scotland's most
famous killer, which showed what Barlinnie prison's Special Unit, in
which he was confined, was all about.)*

*I, as Kay's Chairman at the Supplementary Benefits Commission,
was writing occasionally to her, and in November she invited me to
come and visit, offering hospitality in the way poor people often do. After
walking me around the neighbourhood she cooked an excellent steak for
our supper, which must have been paid for by foregoing other meals, and
insisted I sleep on her bed while she slept on the floor in another room.*

*At Christmas time Kay's three-month stay in Dunning Street came to
an end and she returned to her normal life and home. It was then that a
totally unplanned and unexpected postscript to this story took place. The
BBC decided to make a series of four television programmes about the
people living in one of Glasgow's poorest neighbourhoods, to be directed
by David Martin one of their most innovative directors, and presented
by Magnus Magnussen. David and his team chose Lilybank. It was only*

after Kay was back at work in Glasgow University that they discovered there had recently been a trained observer and eloquent speaker living in this neighbourhood. Although it had never been her intention to make her experience public, when asked if she would participate Kay decided she should help to give her Lilybank neighbours a voice in these programmes. She played a large part in three of them. Most of her audience – including her Lilybank neighbours – were moved and impressed. Many years later I witnessed occasions in the streets of Glasgow when she was approached by complete strangers who recognised her distinctive voice and said, with warm approval, 'You're the Lilybank lady, aren't you?'

But others were critical – most of them graduates living and working on the other side of town. It was alleged that the whole thing had been set up 'with hidden cameras' by Kay and the BBC. She had long been accustomed to criticism and controversy and never responded to it, even when the Principal of her University called her in to deliver a dressing down without giving her any opportunity to explain what had happened. Thirty years later, after her death, the 'hidden cameras' myth resurfaced in the Guardian's obituary. But David Martin and his wife Christine became life-long friends.

VI

THE BARLINNIE SPECIAL UNIT

When the death penalty was abolished in 1965, no one thought to prepare the prison service to deal with the small minority of murderers who are so violent and resolute that they cannot be managed within mainstream jails. Fights with other prisoners and with prison officers led to serious injuries and violent retaliation against these men, some of whom were stripped naked, locked in cages and brutally treated. The Scottish part of this story is vividly told by Jimmy Boyle, one of those prisoners, in his autobiography, *A Sense of Freedom* – recently republished in a new extended edition by Ebury Press.

Prison officials and their officers resolved that better solutions had to be found. Those leading this initiative believed they could learn from the therapeutic communities set up in a few mental hospitals – notably the Dingleton Hospital in the Scottish Borders, led by Dr. Maxwell Jones. Kay, who had got to know him in the course of her work as a psychiatric social worker, became involved in the project and took a part-time job for one day a week in the Special Unit that was set up to try out these ideas in Glasgow's Barlinnie prison – Scotland's biggest jail. The Unit started work in

1973 with little guidance other than a few papers on therapeutic communities, written by Maxwell Jones.

Prisoners and staff were to meet regularly – often daily – and never separately. Together they would plan work schedules and visiting arrangements. Prisoners from other jails nominated to join the Unit would be invited to spend a few days there so that the Unit's existing prisoners could decide whether they should join. There would be athletic challenges and an arts programme led by an experienced art therapist. Leading figures in Scotland's intellectual and cultural life were invited to visit and get to know the prisoners.

Jimmy Boyle was not the first prisoner sent to the Unit, but he soon became a leading spirit in the project, working closely with Ken Murray, an outstanding prison officer. Something of the spirit of the small community of prisoners and staff assembled in the Unit can be gathered from an article Kay wrote at the time of Jimmy's eventual discharge.

Jimmy Boyle and the Special Unit
Saints & Sinners, New Society, November 4th 1982, p. 218

The party invitation read, 'Join us for a celebration of FREEDOM, symbolising a beginning as well as an end – signifying renewal as well as change!' It came from Jimmy and Sarah Boyle, his wife.

It was Jimmy's first day as an ex-prisoner. In 1967, as a young man of 23, he had been jailed for life after a classical history of gang violence – and just 14 months out of institutions since his childhood. The judge gave a recommended minimum sentence of 15 years. But in the following six years his violent behaviour in prison brought him an additional 15 years.

That violent behaviour ended in 1973 when he was accepted into the Barlinnie Special Unit. The story is well known: how he was met by Ken Murray, the most remarkable prison officer in Scotland, and offered an opportunity to live without having to fight every inch of the way to retain his dignity.

It was an end and a beginning; the end of the destructive and the beginning of the creative energy. The energy stayed constant – sometimes the air would seem to thrum round him. He discovered the world of art and, through art, gained access to capacities for sensitivity and love, which had been buried under the 'hard man' image.

The party, held in the evening after a day of media exposure, was for family and friends from all over Britain who had allied themselves to Jimmy's struggle. We were celebrating not only Jimmy's personal freedom, but the idea that all human beings have the ability to grow, change and renew themselves. There was for many of us a bonding of experience of suffering, so along with the wine and laughter there were occasional tears.

Jimmy Boyle has been called a thug and an animal since he was at school. He was almost certainly more intelligent than the teachers and social workers who tried to contain his energy rather than help him use it. There are still Jimmys and Hughies and Billys in our schools whose energies are being used destructively. In a bizarre way, this Jimmy was perhaps lucky to be sent to prison, and to find his way to the Special Unit. But no one should have to be locked up for 15 years to find potentialities that could have been discovered 30 years ago.

No one could blame him if he were bitter. He's not, but he's still angry. Jimmy Boyle's anger kept him alive physically and spiritually throughout his prison experience. Unlike most ex-prisoners, he carries no stigmata of false humility. He is not loved by those with an authoritarian and hierarchical view of the world. He tested their systems to the limit and survived – compelling the authorities to give men like Ken Murray the chance of finding new and saner ways of working with prisoners.

The invitation card showed a bird breaking out of an egg. In prison, Jimmy chose the bird as his symbol of freedom. A lot of people will be watching how that bird flies.

It has flown pretty well. Jimmy is a man who would have succeeded in whatever profession he entered. He had the bad luck to have a father who raised him as a gangster.

Kay's social work had dealt mainly with children and young people going through difficult times and with serious delinquents. She knew their stories were often linked and reflected on that and on her own place in that community in a few paragraphs.

The emotionally wounded

I am a member of that widespread family of the emotionally wounded. In saying that I am also saying that I have to acknowledge my links to the mad and the bad. Those among us who have experienced acute emotional pain, particularly in childhood, are part of a family that includes the depressed, the uncontrollably angry, the driven deviants who seek release for their compulsions in ways that horrify and sicken, murderers, and all those who have broken the codes with which our society tries to protect itself. That I am a member of the family but have somehow succeeded in not acting out those powerful and destructive potentials which characterize its membership, is something I have tried and am still trying to understand. If I know anything it is this: the rightness of the anger is unacknowledged, the quest for love is misunderstood and the need to be listened to denied.

On the periphery of the family are those whose behaviour, while damaging, reflects so closely the values of the 'respectable' members of society that it is difficult to know where to place them. These are those who kill and destroy human beings for financial gain. They include the pimps who smuggle women and boys into European brothels, they include those who import drugs which destroy the health and sanity of those to whom they are sold. In a higher social class, but not a higher moral class, we have those who, also for financial gain, in poor countries exploit men and women in their factories. This goes on hour after hour, day after day, week after week, to produce goods to be sold to wealthy countries at minimal prices but great profit to the factory owner. These workers are paid minimal wages, often not enough to sustain their own lives and those of their children. We are entitled to call it slave labour since the workers have nowhere else to sell their labour. These goods are sold in rich countries to those who never think to ask how they can be produced so cheaply but simply rejoice in their low price although they could afford to pay more.

At the extreme outer edge we have those who make great fortunes by their investment in industries that rape the planet or in their willingness to destroy human beings in large numbers for their own gains – not always financial – sometimes simply to satisfy their need for power. This is the group that I am most reluctant to be associated with yet I know that to do what they do they must… be damaged. They can be described as sociopaths or sometimes psychopaths. Perhaps these are people who… are incapable of feeling the pain of others and in that way are not truly human…

The Special Unit recruited Joyce Laing, an experienced art therapist,
to come each week with art materials and encourage the murderers living
there to try their hands at drawing, painting and sculpture. Jimmy Boyle
describes how terrified they were. No one had ever asked them to do
anything like this, and they were men who did not find being laughed at
easy to tolerate. But he resolved to give it a try and others followed.

Kay reflected in a hand-written note on what was going on, placing
her discussion in the context of prisons for women.

Exploring the heart of darkness

Art enables us to explore the heart of darkness in safety. The
structures created by the artist, whether they be the conventions
of the theatre, the limitations of paint and canvas, or the discipline
of poetry, hold us in a web. Within that web we can explore pain
and horror. Art is powerful – it can breach the boundary between
the outer and the inner worlds.

We lose ourselves in the play, we identify with what is happening
on the stage, but then the action changes and we are safely back in
our skins, enriched by having been given a brief glimpse into the
inner life of another human being...

Every woman knows that emotional pain can be turned in on
oneself: scratching, hitting, rubbing, cutting. There are young
women who always wear long sleeves to cover the cuts that run
from the upper arm to wrist.

Why do we do it? Because physical pain is easier to bear than
emotional pain. To reassure ourselves that we are alive when we
begin to lose the sense that we exist.

How do any of us know we exist? Only by communicating with
other people. They are mirrors that reassure us we can be seen,

that we can be heard. We need also to be touched to know that we have bodies.

When a woman goes into prison she loses all the things that identify her – her clothes, rings, personal possessions – all locked away. She loses her partner, her children, her home, her neighbours, the shops she uses. These are replaced by an impersonal institution staffed with women who feel superior to the prisoners and whose job is to keep them quiet.

She is not allowed her previous identity. So she has to take on a new one.

Angie becomes 'the thief'. Terry becomes 'the prostitute'. Margaret becomes 'the murderer'.

When our identity is weak we become the person others tell us we are. Never tell a child she is stupid, or bad, or a thief. Sometimes we become what others call us.

Imagine being handcuffed: let someone try on handcuffs. What do you feel? Frustration, fear, helpessness?

These are the feelings institutions – police stations, courts and prisons – seek to create. Money is not spared in the buildings. They are designed to intimidate; to say 'Here is where power lies'.

They are mysterious – you have difficulty finding your way in them. Nobody tries to make you feel at ease. You have to ask where to go, what to do. No one explains the rules. You have to learn to please; to keep your nose clean, do what you're told.

Once in prison you are truly helpless and dependent. A child again. No decisions have to be made and if you're there too long you lose the habit of making decisions because you have lost your self.

One way of reminding yourself who you are is to be angry – to keep your anger alive. When your back's to the wall you have to claim your right to exist.

I have met stronger, braver, more courageous men and women in prison than I ever met in my university. The great waste of talent among prisoners is a tragedy. It is talent that was suppressed by our educational system. That is still going on today.

The only justification for prisons would be if a serious effort was made to repair the damage that was done in those earlier years. Far from trying to make prisoners ashamed of themselves we should be trying to make them love, respect and be proud of themselves.

Another piece, written in 1990, probably to introduce an exhibition of works created in the Special Unit, explores the theme further.

An exhibition in the Special Unit.

In every country in the world men and women in prisons are living out the pain, the horror, the humiliations, the rage, the frustrated longings which are for the rest of us the shadowy part of ourselves we protect from the light of truth. When, as occasionally happens, they are given access to art materials in a liberating atmosphere these are often the first messages they try to communicate. Symbols and images come tumbling out, sometimes crude and harsh, sometimes sentimental.

Not all of them want to develop past that point but, as in every human group, there are always some for whom contact with paper and pencil, with paint, clay or a chisel and stone induces a buzz of excitement as they recognise a stirring in their inner life. These are the people who begin the journey of self-discovery through art, and who chart their progress through their creativity.

In this journey they may find the first opportunity to explore the meaning of their anger and frustration – emotions that may have contributed largely to their imprisonment. They may also begin to explore their capacities for love, tenderness, even for fear, which have been denied.

In the act of creation the most overwhelming pain of all, the pain of confinement is overcome as their imagination extends itself outside the boundaries not only of the prison walls, but also the mental barriers that life previously imposed on them. In the very act of handling materials like clay, of gaining control of a medium, in successfully completing a task that they have defined for themselves, confidence and self-respect grow.

Every work of art in this exhibition will represent a point in the personal journey of its creator. It will have a private meaning. It also has a meaning for those of us who see it. The artist and the viewer encounter each other in the work. The messages we are offered are both painful and loving. We are offered a unique opportunity to share the triumph of the human spirit. A new perception of the future becomes possible; a process of self-healing is born.

Saints & Sinners, New Society, Vol. 65, July 14th 1983
About murderers

What surprises everyone who meets a murderer for the first time is how ordinary they are. I'm not talking about drunk drivers or domestic murderers – we can all see those as crimes we might have committed in an off moment. I'm thinking of the kind of men (they are mostly men) to whom the judge says, 'You are a menace to society.'

When you get to know them, they are much like the rest of us. Unless they are insane, which is rarely the case, the murderous part of their personality plays a very small part in their lives.

Why did we not learn at Amritsar, at Auschwitz, at Belsen, at My-Lai or in Salvador – that killing and torturing each other is normal behaviour from human beings? We have to be taught how not to do it... and also be given the opportunity to do other equally exciting things.

Young men – particularly if they have been drinking – will kill each other with little hesitation. Or at least try to. Most of the time they don't succeed. If you put them into uniform with a gun in their hands, their enthusiasm to kill has to be restrained with all kinds of rituals called discipline. There is still a certain tolerance of 'high spirits'.

Many people find socially acceptable substitutes. They joust at Wimbledon, engage heroically in football's tribal conflicts. Or they learn how to make a killing in the market; or they stick figurative knives in each other's backs – smash the hopes of their rivals – rape the underdeveloped countries. They stay legitimate, stay out of danger, earn good salaries or make a profit... The universal detergent which gives admittance to drawing rooms.

What we have just seen from the pro-hanging gang in the House of Commons is the politics of distraction. The game is to pick on individuals and groups and blame them; excite the national blood lust with stories of dreadful crimes; throw a scapegoat to the crowd. Hitler used up the Jews so we can't have them. Who will be next? The Reds? The unemployed? Drug addicts? Blacks? Any quarry who will distract attention from the real issues. We can expect a moral panic at regular intervals from now on.

Every sane person now has a responsibility to understand this game, to watch vigilantly for the groups which will be set up in this way, learn the hard facts about them to challenge the myths and the prejudices which will be put about. Let's always be sure who is the murderer and who the victim.

VII

SAYING GOODBYE TO HER
MOTHER AND FATHER

A few months after her brief spell in Cornton Vale Prison, Kay came with me to Japan where I had been asked to visit academic colleagues and give a lecture. Before setting off she arranged to spend a week in a Buddhist monastery she had heard about. This proved to be a life-changing experience. She wrote notes about it every day – often in a state of exhaustion from the heat and the demands made by the routines she had to follow. Later, in one of her books, she wrote a more carefully considered account of the week.

For Crying Out Loud

On a scorching hot July day a taxi set me down at a small Zen Buddhist temple on the outskirts of a village deep in the Japanese countryside. I had decided to explore the Naikan therapy – 'nai' inner and 'kan' observation... The courtesy and love with which I was met by the abbot of the temple, his wife and family and the monks overwhelmed me. Within ten minutes... I realised that I must abandon myself to this experience, shed all expectations and drift like a leaf in the wind.

Within an hour I was installed behind folding screens in the corner of a small, beautiful temple, sitting cross-legged on a cushion, facing a blank screen, with a dawning awareness of the strict spiritual discipline surrounding me. This place in which my life would be concentrated for fourteen hours a day for the next week was called the 'hoza', a term used in Buddhism to describe a place where the Buddha, or God if one believes in God, would surround and see me. It was a private place. ...I was told that I need only share with the monks who would care for me what I wished to share.

She was given the help of a young man who was the only member of the community who spoke some English. Some, but not much. My guide or 'sensei', who settled me in had prepared a translation of the first questions I had to consider. I read that I had to examine myself in relation to my mother from the time I was born until I was six years of age. I had to contemplate what I had received from her, what I had given her and ways that I had troubled her. This seemed a simple task. What memories I had of those years were vividly clear.

Crying had not been allowed. 'What have you got to cry about?' she would shout at me. '*I* am the one who has suffered.' I suppose there was a time when I cried freely, not only with a sense of self-disgust. Perhaps when I was born, torn so roughly from my mother that the incision made by the surgeons to enable my father to penetrate her was torn more deeply into her flesh, I am sure she cried in rage and pain. Perhaps that first Sunday morning we sang a duet as I too cried. I never discovered the source of her rage, but I was often made to feel that I was the source of her pain.

She was twenty-three when I was born and, if the photographs tell the truth, as beautiful as a pre-Raphaelite painting. It was the colouring, my aunts who feared and envied her told me – the pale skin, the great mass of Titian hair, the sapphire blue eyes. They blamed that hair for her temper, those flashes of rage that left them stunned and shaken and were to do the same for me. They were afraid of her. I learnt to be afraid *for* her.

She wanted me to be perfect – that's normal isn't it? Or is it? Before I was born, she told me, she used to walk in Glasgow's Queen's Park, thinking beautiful thoughts so that I would be beautiful.

My tears seemed to be a threat – dangerous. Perhaps they truly were in ways that I do not understand. I only know my father's response to me through the lens of my mother's stories. It may have been that he, whom she loved with a bizarre obsessional hatred, would flee from my sounds of distress as he fled from hers. So, to keep me quiet, she stuffed her nipple into my mouth until I gagged. She was still trying to get me to suck when I was six. She told me it was because she loved me, but I was an evil child who doubted that.

I had felt I was an evil child long before. Small, solemn and dark, by the time I was sent away to a convent school (*at the age of four*) I had given up hope. I had lost my father. I had lost my mother when she left me with my grandmother. I had learnt to love my grandmother but in the convent I had lost her too. Now I had no one…

I didn't cry when I was left at the convent. Instead, I wet the bed. Every night my body wept at the wrong end. Neither did I cry during or after the only visit from my mother that I remember. I didn't do anything… Even my mother's capacity for dramatizing situations when she had an audience must have been defeated when she was presented with the small wooden creature that I had become. For the first time the power was mine not hers. I would not let my mother near me. We were each alone and not together. It was the beginning of the end of my childhood. The end itself came two years later when, at the age of six, I left the convent on a stretcher, suffering from infantile paralysis... *(The rest of this stage of Kay's story has been told in her own words earlier in this collection of her writings.)*

Now, sitting in the hoza, as I meditated on these first six years of my life, I felt myself flooded with bitterness. Perhaps here in this country among people I had no connections with, I could, without feeling guilty, express my sense of having been betrayed from infancy. Perhaps too I could let go my painfully acquired skills of trying to make sense of everything, which seemed to make it impossible for me to blame anyone for anything.

With the aid of a dictionary I prepared my responses carefully. What had I received from my mother? I slowly and ruthlessly listed... anxiety, misery, loneliness, fear, grief, rage. It went on and on. What had I given her? Someone to love of course, it was obvious. But also a focus for her tempers and her dramas. Had I troubled her? I didn't think so. I had always been a good, obedient, submissive child.

When my senses returned, I was ready, smiling. We each performed the ritual greeting of mutual respect and I began. But before the first sentence was finished, he stopped me. 'This word' he said, '*anxiety*. What does it mean?' I was halted in mid-flight and turned to the dictionary. He checked the translation I offered in his and then shook his head. 'Naikan,' he said, 'is not abstract. It is concrete. Let us take the first three years.' He bowed ceremoniously and left me with my little house of cards demolished.

When he returned two hours later, I had prepared a list of concrete words that I saw as utterly boring and irrelevant to my condition. I would, however, see this odd experience through. What had my mother given me? Food, warmth, clothes, shelter. What had I given her? Nothing of course. How could I? What trouble had I caused her? None really. Certainly I had been ill frequently. But most children get ill.

My list was accepted and we moved on to the next three years over the next two hours, and then again the following three years over the following two hours. For the next two days, interrupted only by meals, temple prayers and a highly …ritualised interview with the abbot, my life focussed on these three questions. What had my mother given me? What had I returned to her? And what trouble had I caused her? I could vaguely discern that there were other people in hidden corners of the temple but the strict rules that I must not talk to anyone, nor get up and walk around without a specific purpose kept them as shadowy figures from whom I heard only an occasional moan or the sound of weeping.

By the end of my second day in the temple my house of cards had not only collapsed in ruins, it was torn into tiny useless scraps. Gradually my perception of the world was shifting. Instead of seeing myself and my needs as the fulcrum of all meaning, I was beginning to build up a new picture of this twenty-three year-old who had given birth to me. Under-educated (she had left school at eleven), beautiful, courageous, ambitious, she went through her life trapped in an emotional and self-destructive nightmare constantly running inside her head.

For the first time in my life I began to weep for her and her pain. I saw her life as central, rather than mine. I was no longer the misunderstood heroine of the most important story in the universe. I wept for twenty-four hours and intermittently for the following two days. Before long I was weeping for myself as well, for the pain of our joint lives, for the pain of existence and for her husband and my father, whom I had hardly known and whose time and place of death are still unknown to me. I had the most extraordinary feeling as if the inside of my head had tilted so that I saw my life from a different angle of vision.

This has never altered. In a temple on the other side of the world in the Japanese countryside, I finally separated myself out from my parents. I went through the same Naikan process for my father that I had done for my mother, and then with all the other significant people in my life. When we are hurt by someone we love it is as if we are caught on barbed wire. Each movement to release ourselves causes deeper and deeper pain as we make new wounds, reactivate those unhealed and reopen old scars. Naikan helped me to stop struggling and to see the unrepayable debt I owe to both my parents for their gift to me of life, no matter what happened after that. Somehow the barbed wire has dissolved. I have learnt to weep more easily with friends for joint pain, but for my own I still seek privacy. I now do so without self-disgust or wishing I was dead.

The story is not yet finished. When young, I sought serenity and yearned for maturity. I thought that was how you left pain behind. Now I know that even if we could leave our own pain behind, we will still have to live with the pain of others, their hurts, their sorrows, their griefs. If we pretend those don't exist, we are dead somewhere inside ourselves. But equally if we do not recognise that these hurts, sorrows and griefs can become the source of courage, of humour, and of a blazing, incandescent capacity to love and celebrate life we have missed the point and missed the opportunity of a lifetime.

Among the writings that Kay left me from the years that followed there is a flow of briefly noted reflections, never intended for publication, showing that she worked with ruthless honesty at reflecting on her experiences and her feelings about them. She said in one of the pieces reproduced in an earlier chapter that she was a member of the 'family' of those who have been emotionally damaged in childhood – people who for the rest of their years live on the brink of madness and violence. Her reflections show that she was not exaggerating. The self-analysis glimpsed in these notes and the conversations she had throughout her adult life – some with wise friends, some with professional 'talk therapists' of various kinds – kept her from going over the brink. But it was sometimes a close call.

She had greater difficulty answering questions about her father, but a clarification of her feelings about him began to emerge ten years later shortly before we went on holiday to Zimbabwe, the country to which he had gone after the war. I select from notes she wrote at that time.

Tonight at the age of 68 I cried for the first time in my awareness for my father. I didn't just cry. I wept and rocked and banged my head. I was the three-year-old crying for his loss and the twenty-something-year-old crying for his death. This started... because of a letter that came today following my radio programme, 'Idle Tears'. I have never grieved for my father. I heard about his death because of a casual remark. I had felt guilty because of my failure to respond to his letters and simply put him out of my head. *(He had invited her to come and join him in Rhodesia.)* My next memory is of being asked at an insurance medical his cause of death. I didn't (and don't) know. All this has been triggered off by our agreement to go to have a week in Rhodesia – now Zimbabwe – and visit Salisbury – now Harare. Should I go to visit his grave? Do I believe he's dead, or is it like the three-year-old waiting for him to come back? David asked someone who had known him in India *(where he had been a colonel in the Indian Army)* who said he was 'awful'. I thought so too at 35. But what did I think at three? I must have thought him wonderful.

This was the same man who, when I was ten, wasn't willing to be seen with a 'cripple' and who threatened to whip me for spying on him *(instructed by her mother)*. The man who at seventeen wanted me to leave my mother and go with him to South Africa – who left me nothing in his will – whose wife did not write to tell me he was dead.

He *was* awful – snobbish, ambitious, pretending and aspiring. But he was also charming, read poetry, valued intelligent company, musical, dressed well, attractive to women, a 'ladies' man'. In other words, a fallible human being.

Can I let him go? *She wrote a good deal more about these reflections and the responses she gained from the few people with whom she shared them, and noted:* I realised that David's father's memorial service *(to which we had recently been)* may also have some meaning for me. Perhaps I could use it as an ending for my own father and let him go?

After spending a week as tourists in Zimbabwe in 1995 she wrote wonderful descriptions of our experiences there, starting with the Victoria Falls.

We went there on the first day. It was an absolutely stunning experience and sitting here in the garden at Ardentinny *(where The Old Manse was now our main home)* I hope I never forget it. My nearest equivalent experience was at the Grand Canyon *(which she had visited some years earlier, travelling by herself on holiday)*. I was soaked to the skin by the spray but it didn't matter. Nothing mattered except the visual impact of those torrents of water, shot through with rainbows and sunlight. I went every possible day after that, but nothing can match the first impact although every encounter was stunning. *(Finally)* our last evening and day were spent in a five-star hotel in Harare.

It was here I think I brought together my feelings about my father. All through the holiday I was conscious that I was visiting places where he would have been and places where he would have taken me if I had visited him. I could see that this man was really a stranger to me. He neither loved me nor cared for me. It would have been better in some ways if we had never met. At least in adoption one can hold onto a fantasy that there may have been a father who would have loved you if he had known you. I do not think we would ever have had anything in common. Yet I have to recognise there is much in me that is like him. I hope I can now let this go – put it behind me.

She finally achieved this some years later, recording the moment in her diary. This morning I forgave my father. Quite suddenly enlightenment came. I felt enlightenment. Light flooded my eyes as I opened them to the dawn and felt light with the knowledge that it was over. Sixty-nine years faded in that light. No shadows left – the bewildered abandoned child faded. No more failure or hurt – mixed with anger, all hidden from the self until forgiveness came, bringing knowledge and pity.

FATHER

After your death, but not before,
I threw away the cardboard man
they'd built around you.

I'd heard them whisper.

I didn't want to hear of your betrayals,
Small or large. And they were small,
Or seem so now.

I know you loved me.

They said you weren't serious,
wanting a gayer life than God allows.
They meant their God.

You sang to me.

And my new found photo shows you
head thrown back and eyes triumphant
winner of a sixties play award.

You made me laugh.

A different God would have saved you
and enjoyed you: even loved you
for the gifts they couldn't stand.

You held my hand.

My hand in yours, you taught me
How to love the sound and shape of words.
I miss you now.

I have waited too long to defend you.

Sin and Forgiveness

Kay abandoned the Church in her childhood. But she retained a lifelong sense of moral purpose, searching always for an anchor for her values – first in ideologies of the far Left, then in psychoanalysis, both of which, she said, ultimately failed her. In a world in which the beliefs and rituals associated with sin, confession and absolution no longer have much meaning for most people, how should we deal with behaviour that we find shocking – our own and other people's? She needed answers, both for guidance in her own life and for her professional work. After much thought and reading she resolved to write a book that would address these difficult questions. She knew she would need help from theologians and other academics, but, with universities going through lean times, she felt she could no longer ask colleagues to read and comment on her drafts as she would have done in the past. She would pay her fees, attend classes and take an appropriate PhD – which she did, under the supervision of Professor David Jasper of the International Society for Religion, Literature and Culture. They became firm friends and before long he was quoting from her work in sermons he preached when acting as a locum clergyman. She gained her doctorate at the age of 75 with a thesis that was published in 2003 by Ashgate as 'Sin and Forgiveness: New Responses in a Changing World' – a book that draws on a range of ideas and sources that only she could have brought together. She left Chris Sunderland's review (for 'Implicit Religion', Vol. 8, No.1) folded into her copy of the book, from which I quote his opening paragraphs.

How should sin and forgiveness be understood in a post-Christian society? Kay Carmichael believes that the time has come for us to look for a new paradigm. The 'Prodigal Son' motif has been powerful and remains so to some degree, but this sort of picture is no longer adequate to embrace the complexity of modern understanding. Taking us through some very high profile cases like Myra Hindley and the killers of James Bulger, she notices the power of the media to inflame hatred and scapegoat offenders and builds a case that these things cannot be described as simple offences by individuals. They are also manifestations of deep things about the culture in which the offences take place. Why is it that a Norwegian community, confronting a situation like the James Bulger case *(in which two small boys murdered an even smaller boy)* could deal with it simply by offering psychological help to the offending children?

The societal element of sin and forgiveness is underlined by some very helpful artistic and literary presentations on this theme. Carmichael alludes to the unashamed adulteress of Hawthorne's *Scarlet Letter*, and to Wiesenthal's *The Sunflower* in which a dying SS soldier confesses all to a Jew he has never met and asks forgiveness. Should he forgive? What right has he to pronounce forgiveness to this dying man on behalf of others? Is forgiveness even the right way to think about this?

With such evocative stories Carmichael opens us up to the idea that the paradigm about forgiveness has become simplistic. It is unable to deal with the complex realities raised by awareness that society both determines what 'sin' is and perpetuates and nourishes certain types of 'sinfulness' by virtue of its very structure. She illustrates this by well-researched and emotive glimpses into poverty, slavery in its various modern guises, and the struggle to overcome oppressive definitions of women.

This is certainly a powerful and moving work. I need no further convincing of the need to re-evaluate dominant Christian paradigms about sin and forgiveness.

Sunderland goes on to outline further issues he wishes Kay had dealt with, but concludes:

Nevertheless I would recommend this book to all those who want to struggle with restating tired formulas in language that connects. There is no doubt that we are living in a 'post-traditional' society where all sorts of accepted world-views are coming into question and will not achieve public credibility unless they can restate themselves in convincing shared language. It is this courageous conviction that marks this book out as important and, in a sense, the hesitancy to come to immediate, defined conclusions could also be commended as leaving a necessary openness for the exploration of others.

I hope I may conclude with the last of Kay's acknowledgements, following those for others who played a larger part in her project: I thank my beloved husband David Donnison, source of my comfort and joy and of the conversation which runs, as Jung described love, like a golden thread through our lives.

VIII

A CITY AND ITS PROSTITUTES

When Kay left Glasgow University in 1981 to join Strathclyde Region's Social Work Services, one of her first tasks was to tackle a problem arising from the arrival of a new police superintendent in the neighbourhood, which had long been a centre for prostitution in Glasgow. Local residents had been complaining, and the superintendent responded with a crackdown, which led to more of the women being charged with offences, so they had to work all the harder to pay the fines imposed on them. Some more constructive policy was needed.

Kay set up regular meetings with a leading group of the women, bringing with her a police officer, a woman lawyer and one of her social workers. In time they were able to agree to rules and practices that satisfied all concerned. It was essential to keep their discussions out of the news, but Kay later wrote an article for New Society magazine that was a humane and wise contribution to a problem of social administration that is too rarely discussed...

For New Society magazine, 14th January 1982, p.53

Recently, a 19 year-old girl was remanded in custody for background reports. She had appeared at the Glasgow district court on a charge of soliciting. Having had two previous convictions, she was also described as a 'known prostitute'. When told, after his decision, that the girl was currently breast-feeding a seven-month -old baby girl, the magistrate said, 'That is a matter for the social work department'.

With no further discussion, the girl was driven off to Cornton Vale, the only Scottish women's prison. Purpose-built in 1972, it lies in the Stirling valley, some 40 miles north of Glasgow and 300 miles south of Aberdeen. The baby's father, on hearing the verdict, raced off to the prison with the baby and handed her over to be fed. The baby was allowed to stay with the mother.

Public opinion, stimulated by dramatic headlines of 'THE BABY BEHIND BARS' variety, was outraged that a baby should be taken to prison. No one said that the only sensible place for a seven-month-old breast-fed baby (or any other kind) is with its mother. Few were outraged that a girl charged with soliciting should be in prison. Many were outraged that a nursing mother should be working in prostitution.

The images do not coincide. Motherhood is pure; a prostitute is dirty. What seems difficult to accept is that prostitutes are people.

Glasgow has about 200 full-time and part-time prostitutes. The numbers don't fluctuate much. A few English women come up occasionally, but drift away again. The economy and the climate are both limiting factors. The current recession has hit business. When money is scarce, prostitution suffers like everything else. Clients are fewer and, at an average of £5 per client on the street, it takes a lot of standing, walking about and waiting to make the average wage of £100 per week.

Prostitution has always been poorly paid in Glasgow. A standard joke for years was about the young man stopped by the prostitute.

He says apologetically, 'I've only got sixpence'. She replies, 'That's alright son. I've got change.'

Most activity takes place on streets in the business centre of the city, and has done for the last 60 years. There is no tradition of brothels, no tradition of advertising for special services, no tradition of girls with cars, not many pimps and those amateur.

Most encounters are brief. A version of the French *cinq à sept* has developed, where men working late in offices will come down looking for 'business', and take a woman back to the office block. It must be a slightly haunted exchange while they try to avoid the cleaning women. It was they indeed who identified the practice, because they objected to finding spent sheaths.

Leaving spent sheaths is seen by the more professional prostitutes as both foolish and unattractive. They think it foolish to draw attention to your place of operation, but they also identify with the cleaning women's distaste. They consider it a responsibility to tidy up before leaving. The sheaths can be wrapped in tissues and stored in a handbag. This may seem a long way away from the elegant Japanese women in Utamaro's paintings, carrying a linen towel as they lead their clients away; but the principle is the same.

There are also a few quiet places near the city centre, where men with cars can take women. This can only happen in the hours of darkness. A few women have a flat where they can take men, but the demolition of most of the city centre tenement property has drastically changed that pattern. Redevelopment meant that those women were scattered to the peripheral estates and had to travel back into town to work. The estates are not economically viable enough, nor sufficiently anonymous. Sometimes a man may be brought home for the night, but the distances limit this.

What we can recognise in Glasgow is a provincial form of prostitution which is relatively well ordered and unobtrusive. It resulted in almost 900 prosecutions in 1980 (the city's population is 600,000), based on a mutual understanding by police and prostitutes about codes of behaviour.

This is not new. Law everywhere depends on cooperation between the accuser and the accused. Standards of acceptable justice have to be built up, if fines are to be paid reasonably cheerfully, and sentences served without too much ill feeling. There has to be a rough-and-ready sense on the part of the accused that the game is being played fairly. In Glasgow, police discretion about prostitutes seems temporarily to have shifted in favour of more prosecutions. There is not more prostitution, simply more arrests and harassment.

The case of the nineteen-year-old nursing mother gives one an opportunity to question not only whether she as an individual should have gone to prison, but also whether any woman should be arrested for offering the use of her body to a man in return for money. The law is quite clear: a woman cannot be charged for taking part in a sexual act in private. She can be charged for publicly inviting the act, or for being seen taking money for having engaged in it. She is not allowed to approach a man verbally, nor is she allowed non-verbally to invite the act. If she stands on a street, and she is a 'known prostitute', she can be charged with loitering for the purpose of soliciting.

If a man approaches a woman, he has committed no offence. It is always her fault if she is known to the police. If she goes into a bar for a quiet drink, the barman can be told not to serve her. To be charged, the man has to be discovered having sexual intercourse in a public place.

When convent-bred schoolgirls are seen everywhere wearing provocative slit skirts, and a possible future Queen of England dresses for a public appearance like the Lady of the Camelias, it becomes difficult to distinguish the appearance of the professional prostitute from that of the most socially acceptable woman.

There seems little to distinguish the woman who offers her body for money from the one who offers hers for career advantage, status, or even casually in return for a good meal. The use of the body as a bargaining tool held by women is implicit in most male / female relationships.

This is not surprising, nor should it be unduly condemned. Women are products of a social experience, which can mean for some that only in this area of their lives do they have any sense of power, of any ability to control their lives. 'Respectable' women are often less their own person than the prostitute, because she is more honest. She names the price in advance. It is neither a reward nor a bribe, but an open transaction. She keeps herself and rents her body.

The concept of prostitution is inextricably linked with fantasy. It is dependent on the buyer's capacity to depersonalise the person he or she is renting. We know little about male heterosexual prostitution, except that it exists discreetly for rich women. It will grow as women take on masculine roles, which include turning to sexual activity for relaxation or tension relief without commitment. We are already seeing emergent amateur prostitution among ambitious young men who woo women who have the power to commission work or influence promotion.

Most people, men and women, find the idea of prostitution exciting. For men, the notion of having a woman whom they can ask to do 'anything', even if they don't know what 'anything' is, has a curious power. For women, prostitutes can represent a dark side of themselves that has never been released. Along with the fascination goes disgust. Along with the disgust goes envy. The combination sells newspapers, and we are given the impression of glamorous lives. After all, courtesans have founded some of our 'best' families, as a reward for sleeping with kings and princes. Today, for a clever girl, prostitution is a way in London – that anonymous town – to get out of her own background and achieve upward social mobility, travel, nice clothes, some bits of jewellery, and with luck a steady protector or even marriage.

But it is not like that in Glasgow. There you have to work hard for your money, and take anyone who comes in that violent and alcohol-obsessed city. The work is often uncomfortable, sometimes dangerous. When you go to court, your name will be in the papers and the neighbours will read it and know it's you. Their children may taunt your children. You don't particularly like your job, but you don't know what else to do.

The money earned is seldom saved. Often it is handed out too generously, as if the world's view of how it was earned reduces its value. Fines have often to be raised by a whip-round among friends. Rents are sometimes in arrears, fuel bills unpaid; there can be anxiety about a sick child, a husband who knocks you about. Too much reliance on alcohol, to distance you from the contradictions of your role, is a constant hazard.

Recent attempts have been made in England to form prostitute defence groups. Their aim is to influence public opinion and change the law. Decriminalisation is the goal. In the immediate future we are unlikely to abolish or eliminate prostitution. We know that the male demand for this service is constant. It is stimulated by advertisers, by magazine publishers, by newspapers. Sexual awareness is fuelled by powerful commercial interests.

Prostitutes' clients are not all freaks. There are some who seek a neutral woman because they seek reassurance of their normality, some because they find ordinary human relationships difficult or threatening. Most clients are very ordinary men, often married, sometimes not. Their needs vary. Some men want quick relief from genital tension (perhaps in a strange city); some men's wives may not be receptive because they are quarrelling or she is in the late stage of a pregnancy; some feel it is appropriate to use prostitutes to meet their wishes for experiences they would hesitate to ask of a 'nice' woman.

For centuries, seamen have put in at ports like Glasgow, expecting services to be available, of which sex is one. Most ports have arrangements that cater for those who come on shore; for those who don't, a balance is maintained between dock security and the ship owners' reluctance to allow women into cabins. Ships are often training grounds for very young girls, who can slip on and off more easily, and are more tolerated by the security guards because they cause less trouble.

Another client group are single homeless men, living in lodging houses or hostels where women are barred. They have no civilised way to encounter women who are willing to meet their sexual needs.

We try to pretend that whole sections of our population are sexually neuter. Our prisons are run on that assumption.

The essential argument against prostitution is that it causes trouble when it is practised as a plebeian activity. Then it becomes visible. Members of the public object. What is tolerated is invisible prostitution of the kind that the more affluent clients can afford to buy. Hotel porters or taxi drivers will see it as part of their job to provide either information about where sexual services are available, or to provide a service directly. In some large hotels, a prostitute will be able to use the in-house telephone to offer herself.

These sophisticated and expensive arrangements are not for the *hoi polloi*. For them the street is, as it has been for centuries, the ground of encounter. The quick verbal exchange, a price agreed, all this occurs in a public place, with the risk for the woman of being seen by the police.

The legitimate fear about the effects of decriminalising this activity is that it might remove barriers that at present give some degree of inhibition to the behaviour of both the men and women involved. Sexuality is a powerful force. Every society sets some limits on its practice. The question is always where to set those limits.

Unlike the rest of the animal kingdom, we seem to have no inbuilt mechanism of moderation. We add our imagination to our biology, and that has no limit. But because sexuality has significance for many people in ways quite different from the commercial, they find its public sale as a commodity difficult to confront in their own community.

Boundaries might best be set by the profession of prostitutes itself, in the same way that other professions set boundaries to their behaviour. There has been a constant lack of dialogue among the groups involved. The clients never identify themselves, nor do they make sensible suggestions about how they would want such services to operate. It seems enough for them that they cannot be prosecuted. Prostitutes make a good case for decriminalisation, but make no practical suggestions for alternative controls. They talk as if every prostitute had a sense of social responsibility. This is not true of any group, including doctors or lawyers. Like them, prostitutes would need to accept that certain levels of public order would have to be preserved.

There is no dialogue between police and prostitutes. It is degrading to both that policemen should have the power to arrest women for their sexual behaviour, and it creates a situation that is potentially corrupting for the policemen. The temptation to take a piece of sex for themselves and pass up an arrest is too available and occasionally yielded to. Any chief constable should be seeking ways of keeping the whole business low-key. He should welcome the setting-up of any collective, group or union that enables him to have constructive dialogue with their leadership.

The other question that arises is what involvement social workers should have with prostitutes. Are they really poor helpless creatures, who need saving from themselves and an awful fate? Some of them are. Every deviant activity attracts a proportion of people who have serious problems of personality and behaviour, and lack self-protective mechanisms. The group, left alone, may drift into alcoholism, serious crime and homelessness. They need whatever help we can give them.

Most others are not. For them, prostitution is a job, which they try to do well. There are older women who would like to retire if they thought they could manage on social security and organise a new life. They may need support and help to do that. They may have to make several attempts before they succeed.

Young girls entering prostitution may, after their first encounters, want to get out, but not know how to manage that without loss of face. A non-judgemental counselling service, linked with practical information about contraception, abortion and venereal diseases could be helpful. Scarcity of conventional jobs may cause more girls and women to think about becoming prostitutes. Before taking such a step, they should know more about the hazards, as well as the opportunities. For some, the price is very heavy. For some, less so. The services for older and young women could both be run by a prostitute group, with back-up by social workers.

The women who choose to stay in the business can be helped to take themselves seriously, and to understand their rights and responsibilities. If men or women wish to provide a sexual service in return for money, that choice should be theirs. Those who choose differently should restrain their prurience, and be willing to help discuss ways of organising prostitution in as sensible and humane a way as possible. Official red-light districts, with brothels, are not the answer; they would produce abuses of power. There is no reason why prostitutes should not register as part-time or full-time self-employed, stamp insurance cards, and pay tax. In return, courts, police, housing departments, health, social security and welfare services should treat them with respect, and give them equal access and status with all other citizens. Their behaviour could be dealt with under the law governing the public behaviour of any citizen, and not under special legislation. Imprisonment need not be available to the courts.

It is not beyond our wit to work out a solution to this important and delicate area of social behaviour. Like all other areas of the market, the supply of a service is linked to the demand. Prostitution is not going to go away in the foreseeable future. But we could make a start by demystifying and civilising its practice.

The week after this article appeared, Kay began a regular column for 'New Society' magazine called 'Saints and Sinners'.

IX

SAINTS AND SINNERS

Kay was invited to write a regular column for New Society: a serious but accessible magazine of the social sciences, now sadly folded. She called these columns 'Saints and Sinners' and wrote about 200 of them before turning to the writing of books. I have spliced some of them into earlier sections of this book and here offer this larger selection – wishing I had space for more of these first drafts of history, vividly written by someone who was always present and involved in what she wrote about.

Last 2 paragraphs of Saints & Sinners, New Society, 24th March 1983, p.470 *About the death and funeral of a friend*

We drank a final toast, then made our way back to our own lives. The death of someone we know always sharpens awareness of our progress to our own death... as, on seeing an accident, we drive a little more carefully for a time. In the West, we are becoming more reluctant to prepare ourselves for that experience. As a child, I was taught to fold my arms across my chest before sleeping and be prepared to die during the night.

I heard during the detailed radio chat that surrounded the Queen's visit to the Cayman Islands that the native tradition there is to make their own coffins during their lives and keep them in the house. It seems that one gentleman practices every day by having his siesta in his coffin. How sensible. The way we die is often a continuation of the way we have lived, just as on getting older we become more like ourselves.

(Kay had her own coffin made, in the form of a bookcase full of books, which stood in her study.)

Saints & Sinners, New Society, 20th January 1983, p.104
About nature cure and the Kingston clinic

The 1960s produced many bizarre phenomena. One of these was the growth of health hydros. They were set up in country mansions surrounded by parklands and grand entrances. They catered for the affluent who ate too much, drank too much, neglected their bodies, believed in miracles and had a masochistic streak.

In them you could be handled by masseurs, steamed in machines, assaulted by jets of water, bathed and starved. You could, in the remaining time, read, sleep, watch television and be bored out of your mind. After a week of this treatment you felt marvellous, looked ten years younger and, several hundred pounds poorer, went back with a clear conscience to doing whatever it was that had been destroying you.

These establishments are corrupt descendants of a movement for natural health that grew up in this country in the early part of the [20th] century. Its founder in Scotland was a charismatic character called James C. Thomson. As a young man he had cured himself of T.B. with a regime of water treatment, physical culture and diet reform picked up from pamphlets written by health 'cranks'.

Nature cure was not merely about health. It incorporated principles of high thinking and simple living, and the idea of reform. It challenged the authority of the professionals, and offered a more innocent and moral way of life. For these reasons it was attractive to the early Fabian and pacifist groups who embraced vegetarianism and teetotalism along with their socialism. Any peace march today will still have to make special arrangements for vegetarians.

In 1939, 'J.C.', as Thomson became known, opened the Kingston Clinic in a suburb of Edinburgh. [*After a long life – and J.C's death – it has now been closed.*] It has the classic characteristics: a small mansion house, a splendid drive, parkland. It was the best surviving example in Britain of the principles of nature cure.

The house is warm and comfortable, the regime is simple. The important offering is the philosophy. They believe that the body, given half a chance, will heal itself. Their job is to help it do that by improving circulation, reforming diet and teaching recognition of the messages the body is trying to communicate when it produces symptoms. Like all good teachers, they believe that no one can be taught anything; they can only be helped to learn.

If the N.H.S. had learnt from nature cure in the way that the Germans and Russians did, it might be facing fewer difficulties today. If more people could go to Kingston instead of hospital, they would be healthier and the taxpayer would save money.

In a health centre in Wales recently, I looked into a mirror and saw a printed message reading: 'This person is responsible for your health and happiness'. That's one of the most important and hardest lessons we all have to learn.

(And she had this message, neatly written in her own hand, on her bathroom mirror for the rest of her life.)

Saints & Sinners, New Society, 22nd March 1984, p. 459

About the early days of the gay switchboard in Glasgow

The rule is to let the telephone ring three times before answering. This gives the caller time to take a deep breath before hearing the words, 'This is the Glasgow Gay Switchboard. Can I help you?'

Even then some people hang up without speaking; or hang on without speaking for something like 15 minutes. Every switchboard counsellor learns to talk into that void, sending out messages of reassurance and concerned interest.

When a caller does talk, counsellors may find themselves responding to a stranger in town looking for the gay bars, or a desperate husband and father facing the prospect of having to drop the mask within which he has lived, or a young woman wondering if the reason she doesn't like being touched by men is because she dreams of being touched by another woman. Or jeering obscenities.

I didn't know there was such a thing as homosexuality until I was an adult. I knew there were things human beings did to each other's bodies, men with women, women with women, men with men (and with animals). But I had no words for these things. They were never discussed. When I did hear the word, I was told there were no working class homosexuals. It was a depravity confined to the upper classes, who corrupted each other at English public schools. Any vestiges of these thoughts vanished as I sat with two counsellors in the tiny windowless room where they take calls.

Homosexuality may be fully accepted in towns like Brighton, in professions like the media, and in places like the law courts. But fear and prejudice are alive and thriving in the industrial working class. Telling your parents, or worst of all being discovered by them, is an agonising experience and can still result in being turned out of the home – as pregnant daughters once were. But worst of all is the sense of having let down, of having failed, someone you love.

The switchboard can only afford to open for three hours every evening. Some nights nothing much happens. On others, waves of pain, loneliness and fear pour down the line. The counsellors are giving of themselves all the time, as well as information about the best bars, and about the ways bodies work – accepting the ranges of normality in behaviour and fantasy.

What sustains them is not just their brief training or their comradeship, but two important qualities – their humility in the face of feelings they have themselves confronted; and their hard-won confidence in their own right to be themselves, no matter what the world may think.

In the early days of what was called The Scottish Minority Rights Group (some years before this article) Kay gave them support on public occasions and helped them to select and train the people who manned their switchboard. As always, there was opposition and criticism, not only from those prejudiced against gays and lesbians but also from some among them who thought such help should be given only by someone who shared their gender and sexuality. She was always prepared to criticise those in the movement who overstepped boundaries she felt to be important – particularly those who tolerated paedophiles.

Saints & Sinners, New Society, 17ᵗʰ May 1984, p. 290
About Kay's childhood crush on a beautiful girl and the later destruction of that girl, first initiated by a gym teacher

When I was twelve, my best friend was seduced by the gym teacher. She was two years older than me, as beautiful as I was plain, as blonde as I was dark, as agile as I was clumsy and for a whole summer she had been the centre of my world. I didn't understand, or try to understand what had happened to me. I only knew that with her the sun, moon and stars were held together in a proper tension, that a wound in my life had been healed.

We were both innocent. Although I already saw myself as the holder of precocious knowledge, it was not in this dimension. We never touched. But I would try to imitate her trick of raising only one eyebrow, and laboriously copy out poems by Elizabeth Barrett Browning rather than risk showing my own less skilled but equally passionate paeons.

It ended in the autumn. We went back to school to find the newly arrived Miss Rennie, in her little black gym tunic and long black-stockinged legs. She invited my love for afternoon tea and advice on her future as a gymnast. She had her in bed before supper, and I learnt that treachery is not the prerogative of men.

I remembered all this when reading the latest offering by Stramullion, the Scottish-based, feminist publishing collective. It is a first novel by Ellen Galford about Moll Cutpurse, a lesbian and sometime transvestite, who was a remarkable Elizabethan pickpocket, fortune teller and sinner. The book is a gentle, loving, informed evocation of the lives of women in 16th century England, told by Moll's imagined life-long friend and lover, Bridget, a herbalist.

Moll and Bridget have a series of adventures and encounters which succeed in showing women's strengths, without making all men fools and villains... though the women tend to be nicer, sharper, more humane. More important, their relationship is depicted without voyeuristic pornography. Bridget describes their sexual encounters with the loving reticence that any decent person would use about someone important to them. The book has integrity. Delightful illustrations too.

It gave me hope. It moves feminist literature forward and makes a lesbian relationship an integral part of, but not the reason for, writing a good novel. I wish it had been available all those years ago. My best friend moved on from the gym teacher to other women, constantly having to cope with racking guilt and outraged family. She was destroyed. I still mourn her and remember that summer.

Saints & Sinners, New Society, 21ˢᵗ March 1985, p.453

About the difficulties of combining a political life or heroic mission with family loyalties – relevant to her own divorce

Within the same week I read Mellow's new book about Scott and Zelda Fitzgerald, *Invented Lives,* and saw the new play by Archie Hind, *Shoulder to Shoulder,* about John and Agnes Maclean. Many people know about Fitzgerald, that more than talented – but not quite brilliant – recorder of America's frenetic Jazz Age. They probably know also that he drank too much and that his wife went mad.

It is unlikely that many people south of the border will have heard of John Maclean (unless they read this column). He was a Glasgow man of Highland extraction, a great teacher of economics, Marxism and the class struggle, whose classes in the City Hall attracted 1,300 to each session. Arrested for sedition in the First World War, he spent years in prison, which destroyed his health. Lenin appointed him the first Bolshevik consul to Scotland. He died at the tragically early age of 39.

Archie Hind's carefully crafted play is based on letters exchanged between Maclean and his wife. Little has been written about the dilemma of the married hero. In a conversational exchange between Maclean and his doppelganger, the central question emerges: are marriage and heroism compatible? The Roman Catholic Church decided a long time ago that celibacy and freedom from domestic ties gave a freedom that was essential to the role of the priesthood. For political heroes, the assumption has been that their wives will support them unquestioningly, not make any demands, nor allow their children to do so.

Agnes Maclean, finding herself married to a priest of the revolution, challenged that view and finally she took her children and left. Maclean's enemies were quick to use her defection against him. Their mutual pain is conveyed movingly in their letters, but no compromise was possible until she came home to be with him when he died of his excesses of virtue.

Zelda Fitzgerald might not have gone mad if she had as much courage. Herself a very talented woman, she was caught in a symbiotic relationship with a man who exploited their joint lives ruthlessly in his driven search to become a literary hero.

Both these couples were products of the twenties: the Fitzgeralds of the affluence, the Macleans of the poverty and injustice. Mellow's book ends depressively on a falling note of the futile waste of their gaiety and talents. Hinds' play ends with the thought that we need Maclean back today. I think we need a redefinition of what makes a hero – or, perhaps more important, a heroine.

Saints & Sinners, New Society, 8th August 1985, p.210

About Maxwell Jones' therapeutic community, a Conference, and the uncertain distinctions between sanity and madness

When Maxwell Jones, founding father of therapeutic communities, came in the late 1960s to Dingleton Hospital in the Scottish Borders and shoved, coaxed and cajoled it into becoming an 'open system', one of the disconcerting effects on visitors was that they had difficulty in distinguishing who was mad and who was sane. The staff had stopped wearing uniforms.

The security guard I encountered at the Brighton Centre where WFMH/MIND were holding their world congress, Mental Health 2000, would obviously have thought that a great mistake. I felt he would have liked us not only to wear badges, but to have 'good' or 'bad' permanently tattooed on our foreheads.

It may be inevitable after the bomb threats that paranoia rules, but I had the uneasy feeling that that kind of society suits some people. It was an ironic comment on the conference since frequently the inner world of madness seemed less awful, less destructive and less sterile than the way in which we sometimes function in the outer world.

The most powerful energy at the conference came from the past and present consumers of mental health services. They talked forcefully but without venom about their experiences of being dehumanised and deskilled, debated the value of professionals, and seemed unanimous in their rejection of medical domination of the services that offer treatment.

The main difficulty for delegates was choosing from the rich and varied menu being offered. There were no taboo subjects and thankfully there seemed to be a minimum of CV-hungry academics presenting research to which the only possible response was – 'so what?'

Apart from Dorothy Rowe, the psychologist, whose book on depression and the nuclear threat is to be published this autumn and who took a special session on mental health and international conflict, the most interesting people there were not necessarily giving papers.

When the gods of madness dance and flicker in our veins they seem to recognise no barriers of language, race, colour or religion... or academic qualifications. But many of us are wearing mental uniforms.

Saints & Sinners, New Society, 29th November 1985, p. 375
About Dorothy Rowe and Forgiveness; her childhood and her forthcoming thesis...

Since reading Dorothy Rowe's book *Living With the Bomb* (Routledge & Kegan Paul, £4.95) I have been puzzling about the mechanics of forgiveness. I should explain that she says, among many other interesting things, that the human task now is to learn to live without enemies. And this means forgiving the enemies we have.

It's an ancient message – none the less powerful for that – but not much put into practice in daily life. The phrases 'So sorry', or 'Do forgive me', are constantly used in upper middle class settings. But they are produced as mechanically as the cuckoo in a cuckoo clock.

There are many other places, however, where to say you are sorry or to make any form of apology is totally unacceptable. It's very much an internal characteristic of talk among *macho* groups like members of the armed services. But it is also a feature of the relationship between government departments and the public. The police, the prison service, the army, the DHSS, the government itself, seem never able to say, 'We're so sorry, we made a mistake.'

It may be that to admit vulnerability is too dangerous. We might be found out in all the other errors we have committed and lose people's respect. So we try to cover up being found out, and being found out becomes itself the sin. The sinner is then cast off and preserves the sanctity of the organisation by becoming the scapegoat.

The point of all this is that unless you *can* say you're sorry for something you've done, no one will try to forgive you. They can only be angry with you... And angrier still if they think you're the one who ought to say sorry. Unless – and here we get into deeper water – we try to understand why that person did the things that damaged or hurt us, and accept our hurt, really let ourselves feel it and then practice forgiving them.

All I know is that it's not easy but it's very important that we try. Unforgivingness damages us more than the person we can't forgive, and we all carry residues it would help us to get rid of. We should have the opportunity to learn about repentance and forgiveness from early childhood onwards; by being forgiven by our parents, by them giving us the opportunity to forgive them and by seeing them forgive each other. But how many of us have been so lucky?

Where today do we find the archetypal symbols to help us through those painful experiences? Some of the women's magazines deal with these questions in their letter pages; some congregations may hear it from the pulpit; counselling services are constantly trying to cope with it. But nowhere does a message come from the powerful in the land. Is that how one becomes powerful – unforgivingly? What does that mean for the rest of us?

Saints & Sinners, New Society, Vol. 60, June 17th 1982, p. 472
On children and incest

In Scotland we have slowly got used to words like homosexual, lesbian, and contraceptive being said openly in public rather than whispered in private. Just recently we have learnt to hear and say another one. Incest. A taboo word. A taboo subject. Not any more. A book has been published, *Incest: Fact and Myth,* by Sarah Nelson, who first encountered the reality when she helped organise an appeal for the Belfast incest victim, Noreen Winchester, who was imprisoned for killing her father, and released after a public campaign.

It is appropriately published by Stramullion, a Scottish-based publishing collective, and reflects vividly the ugliness and cruelty of an almost untouched patriarchal society. It asserts that not only are women seen as the property of their husbands, but so are their girl children. If the women for any reason fail in their role of giving a sexual service, the girl children are forced into the role.

Pre-pubertal children have long been a focus of sensuality. Thomas Mann described it for boys, Nabokov for girls. For several months our classier magazines carried advertisements showing little girls weighed down with expensive jewellery. Child pornography flourishes. Where child prostitutes are available they command high prices.

The book contains a devastating litany of the damage inflicted on children, both physically and emotionally, and an equally devastating attack on the professional helpers in medicine and social work who have failed to take it seriously. A variety of myths have grown up to make this possible. Mothers are blamed for collusion; incest is accepted in the sub-culture; the victim encouraged it.

The facts are that in more than 90 per cent of incest cases that become known, one partner is a girl child of eight or nine, the other is a grown man, who is usually her father. 'Incestuous fathers are not confined to lower-class men; they include judges, professors, doctors, ministers and policemen. They often use violence, threats, blackmail...'.

This is all terrible, but what Sarah Nelson fails to identify is that sexual abuse is only one of a range of violent acts parents inflict on their children, some physical, some emotional. Child-guidance clinics offer a service to many children whose parents may never have assaulted them physically, but they are desperately damaged. We return constantly to the fact that children, whom in this country we are supposed to love, need to be protected from us. We beat and batter them in their thousands, we kill them in their hundreds, and now we are realising that we sexually assault them in their hundreds also. And we do all this in private within the family, which we are always being assured is the cornerstone of the values of our society.

The problem is not only one of incest. The problem is of abuse of power. Incest between peers, whether they be brother and sister, or father and adult daughter, or mother and adult son, insofar as peer relationships are ever possible, is a private matter of religion, social custom and practice. The abuse of power should never be private. It affects all age groups but children are particularly vulnerable. Adults can form trade unions to defend themselves. Children can't do that.

Ours is the first generation that has confronted this problem of protecting children. Until now they have been seen as their parents' private property. It is an important stage in our transition to some kind of civilised lifestyle. Tonight when you lock your door, think what may be happening to children behind other locked doors.

Saints & Sinners, New Society, Vol. 61, July 13ᵗʰ 1982, p.103.
Although Kay's S&S column provoked a continuous small flow of critical comments, she never responded in any way to them – apart from this occasion. I am reprinting only the opening paragraphs of one of her next columns.

I wrote a column recently about incest, which has aroused a reaction in some men who ask to be dissociated from the strictures I seemed to place on them as members of the ruling class of a patriarchal society.

There are only two classes in that society: men and women. These men claim, with a mixture of distress and anger, that under no circumstances would they violate their girl children; that they were equally angry, as women were, with the judge who said that any young woman hitch hiking late at night was 'asking for it'; and that their sexuality is well controlled and dependent on mutual respect, caring and agreement. What is perhaps more important is that they do not want to be made to feel guilty if they affectionately cuddle their daughters or to be seen as potential rapists if they offer a young woman a lift.

It was important for me to be told that. Those of us who feel passionately about the vulnerable tend to exaggerate. This is because we often find parts of ourselves in the victim, our own vulnerability flared up by descriptions of injustice and abuse of power towards others – women have particular difficulties and particular strengths in writing about these matters. ...

Saints & Sinners, New Society, Vol. 62, October 28ᵗʰ 1982, p. 174
On Hallowe'en, death, and her grandmother

A friend of mine boasts of having met a man who, as a child, had seen an old woman being buried in a barrel because she was thought to have been a witch. The dark side of life fascinates us. Every year at Hallowe'en we re-enact some of the drama.

My door bell will ring constantly on Sunday evening. Small groups of nervous, excited, weirdly-dressed children will be standing there, ready to come in and perform a party piece in return for nuts, apples and with luck, a silver coin. My role will be to placate evil and pay off the dark spirits.

My grandmother had another version. For her there seemed to be no barriers of fear between the worlds of the living and the dead. Every Hallowe'en, before going to bed, the fire would be made up, a clean white cloth put on the table and bread, water and salt ceremoniously laid out. I was told in a matter-of-fact way that this was hospitality for the souls of the dead. For this one night, they were allowed to return to visit the world of the living. They would come between midnight and dawn, and it was important to be prepared for them.

I slept with her in the hole-in-the-wall bed in the same room where we lived and ate during the day. So that night I would try to stay awake to see our ghostly visitors. I never managed to and when I woke in the morning, the table would be cleared and laid for breakfast. It was only when I visited Mexico as an adult and learned something of their ritual links with the dead that I realised my indoctrination was part of a worldwide tradition of duties and obligations that reach beyond death.

These gentle rituals have largely been maintained by women, yet the notion of the bad, horrible and ugly witch is the one which is superimposed on Hallowe'en. In the old Celtic calendar, it was indeed a festival of witches, but these witches' 'crafts' were based on the old fertility religions.

Death and fertility are closely linked. Men may kill and fertilise, but women have been left to manage and organise the consequences – the laying out of the dead, the birth of children. These are awesome and magical activities that carry their own kind of power. In the last 40 years women in 'advanced' countries have been giving up these powers. Few people now have their eyes closed for the last time and their bodies washed and laid out by one who has known and loved them. But women are reclaiming power over birthing, and sharing that power with their men. Perhaps we can do the same for death: bring it back into our lives; retain the awe but cast out the fear.

As the proportion of aged amongst us increases we are going to be more aware of death and dying. We will need more than nuts, apples and a silver coin to buy our way out of the scientific magic of preserving life. Perhaps we need a new Hallowe'en festival that will symbolise death with dignity – a witch we can learn not to fear, whose mask may be awesome but not ugly.

Saints & Sinners, New Society, Vol. 62, 18th November 1982, p.302 *On homelessness*

We arranged to meet outside Woolworths. Willie is uncomfortable in offices, and he frightens the staff. Woolworths is a good place. If either of us is late, the other can hang about without looking too conspicuous.

This time we were both punctual. I saw him coming down the street, still cocky in spite of the damaged leg that a knife cruelly gouged; a back fractured by being thrown out of a window; a crooked jaw that never set properly after being broken. He was as clean and tidy as he always is, in spite of sleeping rough or in model lodging houses.

We first met 25 years ago. He was in borstal. I was in my first social work job. Through the years we've struggled on, each of us making mistakes – but his more public than mine, since they took him to mental hospitals and prisons. He's middle-aged now, no longer able to get the occasional job that would lift him, for a time, back into the world of 'normality', no longer as able to 'pull the birds' and get, if only briefly, a bit of tender loving care.

He's depressed, but one thought keeps him going. He's got the chance of a house, thanks to a remarkable example of cooperation between the district housing department, the Strathclyde social work department, and voluntary organisations concerned with the single homeless. These bodies, plus pressure groups, the health service and social security people, all work together in the Glasgow Council for Single Homeless.

At their annual meeting this month, held in a lodging house with residents attending and asking questions, the chairman of the council – David Donnison – described what had been achieved. Over 500 ex-hostel users have been rehoused: very few problems have been reported, and three out of four of them neither required nor received any special help whatsoever. The Council has constantly stressed that single homeless people are not specially handicapped: they require accommodation, like everyone else.

How did they know? They listened to what the single homeless said.

The Council has become a forum at which policies and programmes are drawn up. It is asking for a centre to provide advice, shelter and more coordinated help for the single homeless. *(Set up soon after, named the Hamish Allen Centre and still working.)* It has opposed the district council's commitment to consult local residents before housing people in group tenancies. It has pointed to evasions of the Rent Acts, from which the homeless suffer.

Willie won't be one of the 75 per cent who don't need any help. We sat in a café talking about what it would mean – budgeting; going to sales rooms to buy what he needs; trying to keep his temper when he feels that someone's getting at him; keeping up his Alcoholics Anonymous meetings; using his allocated social worker. It is a formidable set of demands. What gave me hope was his motivation. 'I want a place where I can go in', he said, 'close the door behind me, and know that no one has any right to come in unless I want them to'.

Saints & Sinners, New Society, Vol. 63, 3ʳᵈ March 1983, p.343
On the English Labour Party

In the north there is little surprise at the result of the Bermondsey by-election. Not just because Peter Tatchell is an exotic transplant, not just because he's young and trendy, but because he was represented by the media and his opponents, from the beginning, as a revolutionary socialist. No matter how hard the laddie tried to disguise it by smiling, talking with a working class accent, giving Michael Foot a helping hand up to the platform, there was a suggestion that he had snow on his boots and red gold in his pocket.

How long will it be before we understand that the English working class, particularly the southern English, don't want socialism? If it hadn't been for the Scots and Welsh, they wouldn't even have had a Labour government. They want continually rising standards of living (not caring at whose expense), no hassle, the occasional happening like the Falklands (that reassures them they are superior to everyone else), and, of course, the royal family as their built-in soap opera.

Because, unlike the Scots and Welsh, they haven't been occupied for nine centuries, and were an imperialist power for five – some think they still are – they don't understand the politics of oppression and find it, as yet, impossible to identify with the oppressed poor, blacks or women. They leave that to the middle class.

On this base, the English have been able to develop a middle-of-the-way approach that has great strengths. They have avoided civil wars for three centuries, staying stable while Europe was in flames. Their security and stability made it possible for them to be superficially democratic, play host to refugees – particularly if they were middle or upper class – and tolerate eccentrics. They developed a gift for yielding to working class demands a split second before violence could erupt, and then boasted of being reformers. Compromise developed as an art.

The Labour Party never challenged this tradition. They created their own squierarchy and paternalism. They 'gave' the electorate the health service and public housing, along with treats for children and pensioners. They de-politicised issues by asking not for ideas, but votes. 'Trust daddy', they said.

The English still don't seem to realise that their world is collapsing around them. The SDP (*Social Democratic Party*) is merely another attempt to deny this. The fact is that no one has the answers to our current problems. We have to work them out. People do not seek change – they are usually forced into it, often by suffering.

Political awareness, like personal awareness, comes only through struggle. That's what took people as far as the Labour Party. Labour now seems to have abdicated radical thinking to the Conservatives and the SDP. But I still find the Tories and the Social Democrats more frightening than anything Peter Tatchell has said.

Saints & Sinners, New Society, Vol. 64, 26th May 1983, p.304
On political activism at election time. The election, won by the Conservatives, when Neil Carmichael was defeated by Roy Jenkins for the constituency in which Kay had long lived and worked

For the candidate the election may be about speeches and policies. For the activist, it is about having enough elastic bands to hold the leaflets together. Setting up a committee room is a skilled job. In my part of the world, the agent finds empty premises – usually shops – in various parts of the constituency, and hands each over to a sub-agent. They then run them like little businesses, with the difference that all the work is voluntary.

Styles differ. Some sub-agents insist that the place must be scrubbed out before anything else is done. Others cheerfully import tables and chairs and sit people down to address envelopes with rubbish swirling round their ankles. The first kind usually marks out a corner for himself and the telephone and labels it

PRIVATE. The other kind will always have tea available, and whoever is nearest answers the phone.

They both have their strengths and weaknesses. It is reassuring to be told promptly which streets have still to be canvassed, and to be de-briefed in a way that convinces you that the elderly lady with the bad leg, three floors up, will really have a car waiting for her at 11.30 am on polling day. On the other hand, it's great to be welcomed as if your contribution is going to make the difference between victory and defeat, and to be told that latest local joke about Roy Jenkins. It improves the quality of your canvassing, too.

This time there is no shortage of competent and friendly people to 'man' (yes, that sexist term is still used) the rooms. The unemployed have, for these few weeks, the opportunity of feeling useful and engaged once more. For some it is a baptism into politics – they never 'bothered' before. Leafleting in a shopping centre I was asked by young people where the committee rooms were. I haven't had that experience for a long time. Nor has the impact of the nuclear issue ever been so powerful. The bomb is talked about by young mothers in the same way that unemployed men talk about their mortgages: with a restrained panic.

Leafleting sharpens your perception of the world. You can spot the shopper who is going to try to avoid you 25 yards away, and the two of you, if you have time, can then engage in a slow dance that may or may not end in a leaflet changing hands. Sometimes you are pursued. One elderly man stuck his bottle of pop in front of my face and announced in outrage that in the last week it had gone up by a penny.

Satisfaction comes from feeling that you have influenced the result, just a little. A drunk man wove his way up to me and poured out a fluent argument for voting SNP. I listened silently as a small crowd gathered round us. After several minutes he stopped, smiled sweetly and said, 'Since we've had this nice wee chat, hen, I'll change my mind and vote Labour', and rolled away. A floating voter.

Saints & Sinners, New Society, Vol. 65, July 21st 1983, p.95
On Danny La Rue and sex

The splendid scarlet and gold Edwardian King's Theatre in Elmbank, right in the middle of Glasgow, is full of memories for me. My mother used to take me to the Gods on Saturday nights.

I went again the other night to see Danny La Rue before leaving to join the demonstrators at Greenham Common. I've seen a host of glittering stars there, but none glittered more than Danny La Rue. He must have cornered the market in sequins. His set and his costume dazzle the eye. But nothing detracts from the absolute concentration that he commands from his audience as he repeatedly challenges them. They wonder, when he comes on dressed as a bunny girl, where he hides his testicles.. He puts that thought into words. The women think, 'If a man can look like that, there's hope for me,' and so he gives them helpful hints.

He comes on sexier and more female than any of the women on the stage with him. But he also manages by some great illusionist art to be sexier and more male than any of the men on the stage too; a marvellous bi-sexual whore who makes himself available to the collective fantasy of his audience. In their imagination, they undress him, sodomise him, suck him, handle him, and he stands there and laughs at them and makes them laugh with him at themselves.

At one point in the show, dressed as a facsimile of Dolly Parton in a tight pink satin cowboy outfit, he made a gesture as if to throw his enormous 44-inch breasts to a man sitting near me. The man threw his hands out to catch them with a heart-stopping look of innocent lust on his face. As he realised what he had done, La Rue threw him a look of loving complicity and the man was able to laugh.

La Rue understands and respects the power of sex more than any other performer I have seen. Although he makes his living out of titillating and exploiting human sexual fantasy, he seems to be both celebrating and mocking the mystery, never underestimating it. His work is in the authentic Brechtian tradition. His songs and jokes say, 'Don't believe what you see, look behind the images. Try to remember the truth, don't be deceived.' I was reminded of Jean Genet in *Our Lady of the Flowers* who constantly tells his readers, 'Remember this is a book you're reading. Don't lose your grasp of reality.'

After a series of impersonations, sometimes hilarious, sometimes savage, ranging from Thatcher to Dietrich, La Rue appeared on the stage as himself, a pleasant-faced, middle-aged man of no particular power. He sang a sentimental song.

As we poured out of the theatre everyone was smiling or laughing reminiscently. I'm sure many were going back to beds that would be occupied with happier and more loving enjoyment of the human condition and its absurdities.

Saints & Sinners, New Society, Vol. 65, September 29th 1983, p. 497 *On Harry McShane, poverty and progressive activism*

A shanty, as we all know, is a roughly constructed dwelling. If we keep the sound but change the spelling, it becomes shanti, which is an Indian word for peace. Put the two ideas together, take the Underground to Govan Cross and you'll find the Govan Shanti. This is a rather fragile structure, propped against a wall, where an international group of young people and some Glaswegians will be living and sleeping for the next two weeks.

Their intention is to share with the people living in this deprived area of Glasgow images of poverty in other countries and information about the amount of money spent on armaments that could be better used. To do this among people who are themselves poor is an adventurous step. The peace and poverty movements tend to draw their support from the relatively affluent.

The shanti was opened by Harry McShane, the redoubtable 95 year-old hunger marcher of the 'thirties, who still travels the country teaching young people in universities and summer camps their socialist history and Marxist humanism. Although he has a scholarly understanding of his subject, his gift lies in his simplicity, his personal sweetness and humility. Like many of the people listening to him, he lives on social security.

In a few sentences he linked the struggle of the poor in the third world with the poor of Govan and with people everywhere who seek peace. To do that without pretentiousness is in itself an art. After he had cut the paper ribbon, we stood in the sun eating boiled rice and drinking milkless and sugarless tea.

Children crowded into the shanti, asking questions, having fun. It took about twenty of them, but will only sleep four adults, two staying awake while two sleep. An urban camp poses questions that you don't have to worry about in a field. There are public lavatories a few yards away, but whether they can be kept open 24 hours a day is still a matter for negotiation.

I was making my way home with a cheerful and hopeful heart when I passed a group of youngsters returning from a football match. They were wearing the team colours of the Glasgow Rangers, who are so sectarian Protestant that they wouldn't even employ a Catholic linesman. These young men were draped in Union Jacks, which they must have been waving at the game.

Like members of a primitive tribe, blood brothers of the young people who amuse us on the last night of the Proms, they cavorted and chanted in the street. The shanti looked a very fragile structure indeed.

Saints & Sinners, New Society, Vol. 65, August 18ᵗʰ 1983, p. 251
About poverty and women...

She came and sat down beside me on the park bench. She had one babe in a push chair, one toddler, and a girl aged four. It was a hot day, and I could smell the poverty on her. The scent is unmistakeable: sweet and sour at the same time, the product of a body that doesn't get bathed regularly, clothes that don't get washed often enough or ever go to the dry cleaners.

The children were sweet and clean in thin cotton tops and shorts, but their poverty showed in their skin and hair, and their wary pinched faces. The park we were in serves at one end a very comfortable residential area, and at the other a poor area of older tenements. There was no doubt which end this family came from, and that day they were on their own. All the other children playing around were clearly well fed, well nurtured and from affluent and confident backgrounds.

Their mother had about her a simple dignity that I found very moving. Her relationship with her children was caring and concerned. She was well aware that they did not have the opportunities she would have liked to give them. Her husband is unemployed. She told me this defensively, making it absolutely clear that it was not his fault. She loves children but she will not now be having any more, and she worries about having had the last baby.

This family of five live in a flat which has no bath, only an inside lavatory. They are buying it, but can't now keep up the payments, only the interest. It's on the second floor of a block of tenements, so everything has to be carried up steep stone stairs. They have no hot water on tap, only a small water heater over the kitchen sink where she bathes the children and washes smaller items of clothing and nappies. Bigger things like sheets have to go to the laundrette, which is becoming more expensive. Her husband couldn't possibly be asked to go there – it's bad enough being unemployed without having to be seen doing things like that – so she fetches and carries for the family.

She has never been on holiday, but when her husband was working they used sometimes to go away for a day with the children; probably on a train to one of the Ayrshire beaches. She has never stayed in a hotel, flown in an aeroplane or even been on a boat. She remembers as a child being taken on a day trip to Edinburgh Castle by the school, but hasn't been back there since.

There was no sense of complaint as she talked of her own life. She expressed no hope that it would improve – only that it wouldn't get any worse. She was grateful for small things like this hot summer, which enabled her to bring the children to the park every day. I don't suppose she has read Rilke, but if she did she would recognise his thought.

'Who talks of victories?

To see it through is everything.'

Saints & Sinners, New Society, Vol. 66, 20ᵗʰ October 1983, p. 124
On disability and drama

Imagine a small theatre company planning a performance, rehearsing and advertising. They are all excited because 200 tickets have been sold in advance. And then, on the opening night, they face an audience of seven people.

There had been no national catastrophe to account for it, no violent storm or blizzard to keep people away. Their conclusion was that the tickets had been bought out of pity because all the actors were disabled. Their company is called 'Graeae' (after the three women of Greek myth with one eye and one tooth beween them). That kind of thing used to happen to them.

This week they are in Glasgow for the premier of a play, *Not Much to Ask,* an adaptation by Patsy Rosenburg from Charlotte Bronte's novel *Villette.* I watched them give a dress rehearsal for an audience, all of whom were either mentally or physically disabled. This is a play about illness, courage, risk-taking, longing for communion with another human being and the attempt to break through the barriers that separate the worlds of the 'normal' from the 'deviant'.

After the play, there was a discussion; sometimes hesitant because of speech difficulties, but unhesitating in its sense of a shared experience of our condition. The message was not only for the disabled, as later performances to mixed audiences showed.

It is a message for our times, filled with symbols of constraint, isolation and oppression.

The play also manages to be funny. The B.B.C. 2 *Arena* documentary portrayed the Graeae as a group whose central focus was their disabilities. That is no longer the way they work. What they now offer is theatre that in its content, direction, acting and sheer style is in the great tradition of Grand Guignol. It also has marvellous music.

Why do we find it so difficult to tolerate people who are physically different from ourselves? Why can't we enjoy the differences? Instead of averting our eyes in embarrassment, or taking sidelong voyeuristic glances, it would be nice if we could look openly, curiously and with interest at the different ways our bodies are put together. We could then help each other out with the bits that work for us but not for someone else, or work for them but not for us.

The Graeae is only a part of a great celebration of the abilities of the disabled, currently being held at Glasgow's Third Eye Centre. All the arts are represented, on *merit*, not out of pity. Pity is corrosive. It denies dignity. No one need feel sorry for the Graeae, or any other contributor to this festival.

Saints & Sinners, New Society, Vol. 69, August 23rd 1984, p.181
On the pagan Killorglin festival…

'We're warning you,' they said. 'Go if you must, but the streets will be running in horse-shit and vomit.' They were talking about the annual festival of Puck Fair, held every August in the small Kerry town of Killorglin in Ireland.

Of course I went; I could not resist the chance to see for myself. But until I had, I couldn't understand the mixture of distaste, irritation and pride with which highly educated, professional, middle class Irish viewed this part of their own history.

They were correct. The streets were full of horse-shit and men vomited fluently all over the place. The town was full of horses brought by the travelling people, as they have been for centuries, to be traded and sold. The pubs were open continuously for 72 hours. So none of that was surprising.

What was much more important was the reason for all this activity: one of the purest pagan festivals to survive from the dawn of history. Each year at this time, the beginning of autumn in the old Irish calendar, men go up on to the ancient and remote mountain of Carrauntoohil and catch a great, wild goat.

He is brought down into the town, lifted high on to a specially constructed platform and, with the population gathered round, he is crowned by a twelve year-old girl already chosen as Queen. He is now King, is fed on the choicest foods and after three days is ceremoniously taken down and released on the mountain.

During these three days drinking and revelry continue unceasingly as his reign is celebrated. Killorglin becomes a medieval town with buskers, stalls, fortune tellers and tricksters. Women, carried away by the music, dance in front of him throwing up their skirts in a gesture that goes back through the centuries. Transcendence is found in all the well tried ways known to human creatures.

But all this goes ill with the image of a nation striving to become a new Sweden. The dirt and the superstition might not be appreciated in Brussels or at the UN. Television cameras have begun to come from all over the world to record this fertility ceremony. Before long the horses will all be herded into a field, there will be litter baskets for ice cream papers (and vomit bags?). The Queen will be offered a film contract.

Then the baleful yellow eye of the great goat will be the only wise comment on a world that fails to recognise how important the dark side of our life remains for all of us.

Saints & Sinners, New Society, Vol. 71, January 10th 1985, p. 69
On Harry McShane at 93

Having abandoned genuflecting to gods, I had no intention of recreating their image in human form, so at political rallies I have determinedly stayed sitting down while people all around leapt to their feet to give a standing ovation. Until last week, when for the first time in my life I stood to applaud and honour a man who has himself eschewed the seductions of public life and any kind of personality cult.

Harry McShane, a 93 year-old revolutionary, was being given the freedom of the city of Glasgow. Even some of the Labour councillors were uncertain about his respectability and suitability to become a freeman of the city. His proposers were thought to be rather radical. But, having made the decision, the council came up trumps. There was a Lord Provost's lunch followed by a reception for an amazing mixture of 200 of Harry's friends ....peers, parliamentarians and the hoi polloi.

After the ceremony he spoke for ten minutes; modestly about his love for his city, challengingly about the need for a new form of labour movement united to change society. He had come into politics 75 years before with that as his goal. He still believes it to be possible. During those years he helped lead the Glasgow workers' revolt in 1920, was imprisoned for sedition, led a hunger march from Glasgow to London, and was a close ally of John Maclean, that other great Clydeside Marxist hero.

After 20 years as Scottish editor of the *Daily Worker*, Harry split with the Communist Party on ideological grounds in the 1950s and, when most people are ready to retire, went back to his trade as an engineer in the shipyards. His engineering skills are probably the only thing this modest man has ever been tempted to boast about.

He never joined another party although many have courted him. He describes himself as a Marxist-humanist and focussed his scholarship on the early writings of Marx and the work of Adam Smith. One of his recent great excitements was to handle, in the library of the University of Glasgow, the original lecture notes of a student who attended Adam Smith's lectures.

While he was receiving his freedom of the city, the red flag flew over the city chambers. If we had more citizens like him it would be there all the time.

Perhaps the reluctant councillors were right to be cautious after all. But isn't it marvellous still to be thought dangerous at 90?

Saints & Sinners, New Society, Vol. 73, July 5th 1985, p.30
A battered mother and Francis Bacon

It was her fragility I first noticed. Every big city has girls like this; reared in poverty, undernourishment and fetid air. They're like exotic, waxy orchids, pale and looking as if the slightest touch would bruise them.

I followed her down to the platform on one of Glasgow's underground stations, she clutching a small girl in her arms – and it was only when standing beside her that I was able to see that she had indeed been bruised. Her right eye and temple had been most fearfully damaged. The flesh was swollen and broken, and she was trying to hide the whole misshapen pink and dark purple area under a fall of yellow hair.

She looked about 17. Her thin small body sagged under the child's weight and both of them were dressed cheaply, but with care. The little one was a miniature of her mother. I was as certain as it's possible to be without hard evidence that she had been battered the previous night by a man. Glasgow, it used to be said, had the highest incidence of wife battering in Europe.

On the previous day, in London, I had been to the Francis Bacon exhibition at the Tate. After an hour looking at those paintings I had come out, as one does after a powerful experience, seeing the world quite differently – seeing people's faces in new ways: in this case their skin just holding together the deliquescent flesh. And for a brief second, when I saw this youngster's face, I thought I was superimposing Bacon's images on to her. But I wasn't.

She carried her bruises and her child away from me on to the next train. If she had appeared distressed I would have spoken to her, but there was no sign of that. She was holding on to her courage and her pride, and my guess is that she was going to spend the day with her mother who would console her by describing her own and other women's experiences of being knocked about.

Perhaps not. Perhaps she'd say, 'Don't allow yourself to be treated like that'. But she might be afraid of the consequences if she did that, both for her own life, because she might have to give her shelter, and for her daughter's safety.

I keep thinking of that young woman. She's all mixed up in my head with the Francis Bacon portraits. You wouldn't think they had anything in common...a wee Glasgow girl and a world famous painter. But they do.

When Harold Wilson formed his first Government he set up a small Policy Unit at No. 10 Downing Street, staffed by economists and social scientists to provide him and his colleagues with advice. Kay was recruited to work for one day a week in this Unit as their expert on social policy and Scotland. She enjoyed this demanding task and made good friends among her colleagues at No. 10, but retained a sceptical view of the trappings of power – conveyed in another of her Saints and Sinners columns.

Saints & Sinners, New Society, June 24th, 1982, p. 515
The pomposities of Parliament

George Thomas, Speaker of the House of Commons, was reported recently as saying that the uniform he wears for his job lends authority to his role as defender of free speech, and that this is especially important when democracy is on the defensive across the world. His working clothes consist of a wig, cutaway coat, knee britches, black stockings and buckled shoes. They freeze his image in the 18th century, a period regarded with nostalgia by some would-be aristocrats, but not distinguished in this country by democratic aspirations.

Uniforms do indeed convey messages. The Foreign Office is apparently nervous about allowing the governor of the Falklands to wear his plumed hat when he returns to the islands. It is feared that there could be nothing more provocative to the defeated Argentines than the display of the symbols and trappings of colonial status.

The police, of course, wear uniforms, as do prison officers until they become really senior and important in the administration, when they are allowed to look like gentlemen. A Scottish group of prison officers suggested that they should wear ordinary clothes while working with prisoners to rehabilitate them. They felt it would establish better relationships and lessen prisoners' anti-authoritarian attitudes.

The idea was rejected on every side. Officers clung to the uniform as a symbol of authority and also as giving them protection, while their seniors saw such a move as a threat to the hierarchy. No one would know who was who, and that was a terrifying thought.

On the other hand, nurses in some more trendy hospitals have escaped from uniform in an attempt to blur the distinction between the sick and the healthy and to democratise the institution. In some asylums for the people whom we have decided are more mad than the rest of us, the staff are not distinguished by their clothes.

So what's with Parliament? If our democracy depends for its survival on an elegant but rather absurd form of fancy dress, that's bad news. Why would any rational institution preserve such a custom? There must be a reason. There must also be a reason why a citizen who wants to communicate with his own MP has to rely on a series of messengers wearing black uniforms with gold badges hanging in front to hunt him down and deliver a message in writing.

Nye Bevan wrote in his autobiography, *In Place of Fear*, about his introduction to the House of Commons – how he was taken round the statues and told the history as if it were his history. 'These were not my ancestors', he said, defining himself as a member of the working class. The Labour Party never learned that lesson. They continue in the person of nice men like George Thomas to be seduced into styles which prevent change penetrating that institution. They look to the past, not to the future, which is hurtling towards us.

X

SOME OF KAY'S POEMS

When stuck in a delayed train without a book to read or in a boring meeting from which we cannot escape, most of us probably doodle irritably on any piece of paper that comes to hand. Kay would write a poem. Back home again, she would bin it or put it aside, but rarely revise it or share it, and never publish it. Many of them will be stored among her archived papers. I have already spliced some of them into earlier pages of this collection. In the pages that follow I provide some more, always following her instructions never to change a word of them. I begin with those her friend Larry Butler assembled for her funeral.

GRAN

I saw her dead,
the generous body
into which I'd coorie
shrunk.
She was ready now
for a decent funeral
at the end of a decent life.
She had taught me
the virtues:
clean clothes,
a clean and tidy house
and loving.
I loved her.
I never said the words
but I think she knew
by the way
I clung to her skirts.
If there's a heaven
she'll be there
picking up feathers
dropped from angels' wings
and washing Jesus' bloody garments.

DEAR GREEN PLACE

Dear green place
I fled you but returned,
explored your depths,
hidden and forbidden,
thought that was where I belonged.
I wandered away
watching others,
learning,
thinking
no one would notice
that I didn't know
how to behave like them.

MY MAP

My map is full of people
full of love and full of hate
safety and danger.
Only in my safest place
are there none.
My safest place is me alone:
no need to please, to give, placate,
put on a mask.
No need to ask
permission to be
myself.

LIFE IS THE POEM

He continues quick and dull in his clear images;
I continue slow and sharp in my broken images.

He in a new confusion of his understanding;
I in a new understanding of my confusion.

Robert Graves

To try is a mistake
it is better
to wander through paths of uncertainty
to taste surreptitiously
to smell the faint perfume
of unorthodoxy
to savour an error
time stretches and contracts
to meet our longings
not to wrap in plastic
the thoughts that conflict.

THAT STILL PLACE

If ever I find it
that still place
I will know it
I see it from
the corner of my eye
every day
but it slides away
as I try to focus
it hovers at the edge
of all my senses
hauntingly familiar
like the homes I never had.

WHERE HAVE YOU GONE?

I know that we buried you
but that's no answer.
We buried a body.
But where did that spirit go –
The passion, the energy,
The quick response.
Age did not dim your pleasures,
None indiscriminate.
You chose whom you loved
You chose whom you tolerated
And allowed to care for you.
I miss you
And wish I had been kinder.
Less impatient and defensive
Of my clean and tidy world.
I even miss
Your incessant demands for food,
Your shiny, flea-ridden fur.
Where have you gone
My ancient scabby, toothless cat?

MY SPIRIT

my spirit
released from the prison
of its own making
soars
an arrow
caught on glittering threads
of spinning suns
leading towards infinity
knowing no goal
seeking no mark
the journey enough reward.

WE

We are a group of women.
We came together in anger
but work together in love.
Anger drove us to resist, rebel.
Weapons and war are our foe.
Love drives us to cherish our land
hold each other by the hand
and say NO.

HOW TO MANAGE YOUR DAUGHTER

My daughter
tells me:
Mother, your hair needs cutting,
your eyebrows need plucking.
I wince and obey.
My daughter
tells me:
Mother. You need a holiday
I'll take you away.
I laugh and obey.
My daughter
tells me;
Mother, do that or do this
and gives me a kiss.
I weep and know why:
she doesn't want me to die.

LOVE IS NOT THE SUBJECT OF PRESCRIPTION

Love is not the subject
of prescription,
not measured out
in grams or even cups
of time.
Not for negotiation –
so much
of this or that.
A stranger to the market place,
there is no meter ticking
out the cost,
no bars switch off at will.
Once lit the fire's life's
Its own.
I only tend it.

EASTER SUNDAY

Irreverence is necessary,
essential,
as we swim in a sea of absurdity
surrounded by strange creatures
and a few sharks.
To take them seriously
is to put our selves and our sanity at risk.
We have to take each small mystery
and find in it
the cracks and fissures that let in the light of reason.
In doing so
the greater mystery will unfold itself
and entitle us to a sense of awe.

REFLECTIONS

I turn away from your faces
and from your souls,
men and women
who sit round this table
debating, considering,
seeking each others'
approval.
There is no disagreement
only modification
and blurring
of dangerous issues.
Fascinated by your own voices and words
you look at each other as in mirrors
which reflect back your own virtues,
intelligence and status,
as you constantly remake the world
in its own image.

I am still a good Catholic.
The sin lies not in the act
but in the intention.
The game is not a game
but played for real.

HAVING MORE TO GIVE

Having more to give than is asked for,
having more to say than can be heard
is a special kind of pain.

The pain clinic said
Right where is it?
Everywhere.

How long has it been there?
The pain emerges
like a seal from the water
sits on a rock in full view
then disappears, but doesn't go away.

THERE IS A COUNTRY

There is a country called denial
Where
All is well
All is always well
Always will be well.
No weeds clutch ankles
No gates are closing.
Pain can be trapped
And placed on a shelf
In alphabetical order

THE BITTER CIRCLE

I am not the woman I was
I said
And in the silence
Pain wound through my heart
as I recalled
my lost innocence.

Then I remembered
that
I am the woman I was.
I have been here before
in the circle
but seeking the spiral.

GOODNESS

Goodness cannot be weighed,
measured or caught in a jar.
Like the vault of sky,
the glory of wind.
I recognise it
and respond.
It can be a smile,
a caring touch,
a hug given with love,
or time, that most precious gift.
Its essence is generosity,
allied with modesty,
underlined with knowledge
of the truth
of what it has to offer.
I met it today
And my heart sang,

TO LARRY ON BEING 60
FROM KAY ON BEING 78

Sixty is young
Bus pass or no.
When I am 80
I will be old –
But not yet –
I have two years to go.
Old is always ahead.
We, you and I,
will never be there.
The decades pass
and we simply learn
the things we thought we knew.
But we will never learn
what we don't want to know
like – how to be old.

TO BE ALONE AND NOT SEEN

How to describe it: the pleasure,
The subtle, sweet sense of relief.
To be alone
To be not seen
To strip inside the head
Naked
No one to care or even notice
No defenses
No courtesies
No need for protection
No suffocating, overwhelming sense of other
No mea culpa
No please
No thank you
Only the self to blame, to please, to thank
And ultimately
But only if one wishes
To forgive.

The freedom then to be self
That creature always hiding
While terrified of not being found.

BEING EIGHTY

Being eighty is no joke,
there is no hope

of going back and changing
history
as once seemed possible.
I'm stuck with who
and what I am
and have to
make the best of it.
No point in psychotherapy,
or struggling to learn
another language.
I'm expected to be
a finished product.
But it doesn't feel like that,
I still feel raw round the edges;
An unfinished piece of embroidery
not yet ready for the frame,
hoping for more colours
to be added.
And sometimes, by accident,
I catch sight of myself,
hanging in a mirror,
and I wonder
who that woman is.
Is it time now
to get to know her
and find those private,
unfinished bits
that will make me able
to see being eighty
as a joke.

And finally, for this series, a poem by Larry Butler that was written for a joint birthday party

LOVERS

For Kay Carmichael and David Donnison
celebrating 160 years sharing this planet
with all of us from 1926 to 2006

Two beings determined
to make a difference,
not cowed by judgements,
open-hearted, friendly, welcoming
all sorts of people & dogs & cats & plants,
champions for change biting the socialist bit
signalling a battle with wealth & inequality

loving the world they live in
living the life they love
lovers of love, wind & surf, music & dance
lovers of peace & justice & art
word lovers with powerful pens
lovers of life & the right to choose
when you die. Lovers by night, lovers by day
falling freely for each other & all of us
& all of us & so say all of us.

More of Kay's poems follow

THE LICENCE

How can I sing for you
If I'm not allowed to weep.

How cry out with pleasure
If not with pain.

How can I shout for joy
And not for rage.

How can I know the sun
And not the rain.

Freely dance
And never stamp my feet.

HELL MAY BE HOT

Hell may be hot
But the church was cold,
An old, cold building

But not as cold
As the body in the coffin
We had come to honour.

She had been
A good woman
In the way that women
Used to be good.
Faithful and caring,
Asking no reward.

He expected her
To care for him
Until his end.

In the last act of her life
She betrayed him,
Dying in the night,
A smile on her face.

BEN THE KITCHEN

The range was buffed into submission
the jawbox gleamed with her pride
the linoleum shone with her anger
no one knew where she cried.

You'll be the death of me.

Into the fender she polished the poison
that lived in her soul and no one could fathom
the reason she even dusted the coal.

You'll be the death of me.

Eating was always a hazard, the last bite
hardly gone down, when she'd say. 'The table's
got to be redded', somewhere between a scowl
and a frown.

You'll be the death of me.

Father could smoke in the lavvy
but still she'd make such a fuss. He'd sneak away
with his baccy, not even allowed to cuss.
If he took the evening paper to have a quiet read
she'd hold it to her nose and say, 'There really is
no need to crumple it, nor to make it smell,
you should manage these things better.

You should control yoursel'

You'll be the death of me,

Hell's made of good intentions, He really, really
tried
To love this spiky lady, but found it very hard.

You'll be the death of me.

A widower from the stroke she took,
his life has really changed, his baccy's
In the kitchen, his feet are on the range.
He buys flowers for the table, he even bought
a rug. But in the lavvy he tries to forget
the night – he didn't pull the plug.

He was the death of her.

A ROOM

There was a room
Where the sun always shone.
Always.
On the window sill
Of that room
Doves always cooed.
Always,

Love lived in that room
Laughed and sang
Danced and dreamed
Ate and slept.
There were dark grapes,
White wine, moist thighs.
Always.

Two dragons at the door
Tamed
By remembered love
Entertained us
Made our bed
Brought flowers to celebrate us
Between tortoise shell walls
And a golden door

THE EMPTY CHAIR
(for the same man)

They told me you were dead.

I did not flinch
but when alone
I set two places at my table;
and food for a loving wake.

I brought two chairs,
set them there,
and, sitting in one,
waited for you to tell me
what I could remember,
what I must forget.

I must forget
The olive taste of skin,
tumultuous beds where we explored
each others' needs and joys,
in secret places.
And knew already
there was naught I dared remember.

So holding high your plate and glass
I ritually let them fall.
The plate broke into three
mocking the rules of love you taught me.

The shattered glass sparkled
like tears I dared not shed.

With equal ceremony
I replaced your chair
against the wall,
remembering to forget
and, I thought, succeeding
until today.

SONG FOR A FRIEND
(Hilda Mchlery)

You shop for clothes like a duchess;
Nothing's too good for your back.
Max Mara, Jean Muir and Armani
all hang on your private clothes rack.

Only I know why it's important,
only I know how you were teased
in the posh school where nuns were to teach you.
You never felt at your ease

for your parents couldn't afford it –
your scholarship had got you there
but the uniform wasn't included and
you nearly gave up in despair. So

your mother did what she had to
in finding the clothes second hand.
The blazer and gym slip she managed,
The blouse, that had to be planned.

And she sat and she sewed it together
With stitching that was neat and true.
The pattern she thought was so pretty,
the colour it had to be blue.

The first day you got there too early,

dressed as you thought in your best,
hoping the others would like you
and see you as just like the rest.

When you heard the first snigger
it had such an ugly sound
and a girl said aloud to her neighbour,
'Her collar's not pointed, it's round'.

UNTITLED

Waking
I saw the moon
lambent silver
in a navy sky
dancing
in and out
up and through
the clouds.
And I thought
of the times
when my urgent womb,
in rhythm with the moon
danced a slow pavane.

EASDALE, JANUARY 2006

For you
I am
the stone on the beach
flowering jasmine
rain on a glass roof

For me
you are
nakedness
melted chocolate in my mouth
the warmth of a bed

We say to each other
here I am, and we smile.

UNTITLED

It was a Glasgow occasion
about which, as always,
I felt ambivalent. He had been
a lovely man, lovely and loved.
The church was packed
and drenched with grief
politely unexpressed,
aware that this death
was premature; unexpected.
The service was Protestant
but not protesting.
To my surprise, I found
myself yearning for some
vulgarity, something to smother
the certainty, the confidence,
the assurance that God,
their God, was one of them,
approving of the Covenant
defending us against
ritual, saints and stained glass.
Relief came with the singing.
The sound battered the roof,
wound round the gallery,
trembled the pews, allowed us
to weep quietly, appropriately.

MEMORIES OF HOUSES

Memories of houses.
Like women
Some beautiful,
Some plain:
All offering gifts.
Memories of rooms.
Rooms for loving,
Rooms for weeping,
Rooms for anger,
Some for comfort.
I wove my way through them
As I wove through my life
Leaving, I hope, a trace,
A faint perfume on the air.

5.1.08

Killorglin is a village on the west coast of Ireland. Every year in late summer travellers come from all over the West, as they have done for centuries, to hold a horse fair. The pubs stay open for the 72 hours of the weekend and what I am describing is the central event of the fair.

THE GOAT

They haul the lax and heavy, pinioned, demonic God
up the high tower, his hot and slanting yellow eyes
glazed by the tranquillizing dart.

We stand, packed into the narrow, cobbled street,
heads upturned and worshipping, although
we would not confess it to the priest.

The black, cleft feet are steady now on nailed together
boards,
his bronze horns, his beard, his coarse and heavy hair
shine in the sun. He is our forbidden risen Lord.

He is our Lucifer. His stench is in us. We yearn for him.
Now a way is cleared
and through it comes a child in virgin white.

No blood as yet has trickled down her thighs. And
up the steps she walks, followed by the priest
and two attendant girls, to touch the goat.

A great sigh runs between the crowd
for she is his bride.
Fourteen hundred years have made no difference,
The corn has still to grow and mares drop foal. The land
needs blood and seed.

The pubs stay open, more seed may be spilled
or even blood.
The tower's taken down,
the goat set free on his high mountain.
In his dark dreams he will remember
that for one day he was again a God.

MEGAN*

Just as your life enriched
so does your death diminish me.
You held my memories
of passion, pain and promise safe,
as I held yours.
These private gifts
exchanged from year to year
are left with me.
When I too die, they'll go –
burned with my ashes.
None to remember
our private selves.
Only the public face survives.

*Megan Browne, Kay's tutor at the University of Edinburgh and
life-long friend.

XI

LIVING YOUR DYING

In 1992, Kay was invited to talk about death at a meeting of The Voluntary Euthanasia Society of Scotland – later renamed 'Exit'. A revised version of her speech was published in their journal in September of that year under the title 'Living Your Dying' and reprinted in their journal in November 2007 entitled 'Images of Dying'.

Our society teaches us little about how to die. Television and films offer images of how people are killed, mostly in violent and horrifying ways, but these images are concerned with the outer manifestations of death rather than an inner approach to the ending of our lives. It was not always so. The history of all religions is also the history of giving a meaning to death and dying, and of finding ways of coping with their inevitability and mystery. That mystery lies at the core of all our lives.

Few of us today have the opportunity to be present at a death or even to see a dead person. Hospitals and nursing homes are where most of us die. We have disconnected ourselves from the dying and are left with neither hope nor knowledge. Friends and relatives, given the choice of seeing the body, often choose not to, saying they would rather remember the person as they were – as if the dead body was nothing to do with that person, as if that same body had not been the focus of pleasure and pain, of joy and sorrow throughout a life.

That was not always so. As a small child my grandmother, who was often asked to help with the laying out of the dead, would take me to see the bodies of those friends and neighbours.. On one occasion I saw a small child of my own age, about four, laid out in a little white coffin on the kitchen table of a tiny room and kitchen house. I was never frightened. For her, a woman of peasant stock, life and death went hand in hand and she communicated that to me.

The social consequences of ignoring the rituals surrounding human death are far reaching. It is important that we treat the loss of life as a significant event. Only in that way can we honour life.

At birth, in being given life, we are also handed the card of death. We have to take both together. It was easier for people like my grandmother who had a clear vision of death's place in the wider scheme of things. It was not an end, simply a passageway to another world; a ritual of passage. She lived in the grand tradition of acceptance of the myths and stories developed by all societies in the attempt to ensure that we, each of us, do not die a meaningless death. For many people some kind of immortality is a prized goal. The human psyche seems unable to tolerate the idea of its own extinction. Empires have been founded, families established, books written, great ventures undertaken by people who want to be remembered. In that way death could be denied.

Our society is at the moment in a dangerous interim phase. We are rejecting many of the ideas of the great religions but have not replaced them with a coherent set of alternative images that will help us to give some meaning to our lives and our death. Our attitude to life is inextricably bound up with our attitude to death.

From birth each of us is on a journey and each of us is living out a story – the story of our lives. In that story each of us is the central figure, the hero or the heroine. Everything that happens in the world has relevance only if we chose to make that so. We are the centre of the universe. It is therefore hard for us to believe that the story will have an ending.

Yet, as Heidegger has said, 'For authentic living it is necessary to have a resolute confrontation with death.' So the task for humans is to strike a balance between our sense of invulnerability and the limitless horizons with which we began our journey, and the vulnerability and doubt that come as we grow older. We need to preserve hope and a sense of meaning while having a realistic understanding of our closeness to the end of our journey. Few of us are afraid of death; what so many of us fear is the manner of our dying. That is the reason we have come together in this society. We fear pain, humiliation or loss of dignity. These are not unrealistic fears, nor are they new. The concept of a good death, of dying well, goes back a long way in human history; as does the notion that we can choose how we die. It may be that the last act of our lives is one that we want to take responsibility for as a statement of the quality of our lives.

There seem to be two fundamental styles of dying. The first is the quick and unexpected death – the car accident, the fatal heart attack. If this can be a clean end, with no recovery that leaves incapacity and dependency, that is what some people would prefer. The other style is the slow death – a long illness with plenty of warning to get one's affairs in order, time to say goodbye to friends and – with a little luck – a gentle death with the family around the bed. Each of us should consider which we prefer, but try to recognize what that tells us about ourselves and about how we want to live our lives. People say they want to be in control as they die, to have dignity, not to be screaming in pain or fear. This may be how they have tried to live their lives, perhaps at the expense of showing their real feelings when it would have been more appropriate to do so.

Some of these fears may have no base in reality but may be remnants of the terror felt by infants left alone to cry for long periods; hungry and feeling abandoned in life threatening ways. We may carry these hidden fears with us through our lives only to have them surface when our bodies once again become vulnerable.

But there are many ways to describe the path to dying. Acceptable or unacceptable, natural or unnatural, passive dying, premature dying, self-destructive dying as with drugs or alcohol. All these terms reflect serious attempts to understand and talk about how and why people die and in what way a death connects to the life that precedes it. That last thought is central to what I am trying to say. The way we die is seldom isolated from the way we have lived. We can die our own death if we have lived an authentic life, we can die someone else's death if we have lived our lives according to someone else's script, or we can die the death of the culture in which our lives have been led.

Our culture offers us a range of mythologies of death. Stanley Keleman who has written widely on this subject characterizes several. The Hero's Death. The Wise Man's Death. The Fool's Death. The Martyr's Death. The Morbid Death. At various times in our lives we have all sensed these mythologies. By bringing them into consciousness we can choose which of them, or even which parts of them, have validity for us. Or we may reject them all and wish to create a new story for ourselves.

In the manner of our dying we can make significant changes in relationships. I saw this with my own mother. Her life had been a complex and unhappy one, very destructive of personal relationships. I had few happy memories, but when she realized that she was dying she applied herself to doing that well. I am constantly grateful to her for that. Her death also taught me that death need not be tragic. It can be a relief and a joy both to the person dying and to their family. We have been conditioned to see it always as tragic. If we allow the possibility that it need not be so we can have a wholly different feeling, not only for another's death but also for our own.

A friend of mine told me this story. Her mother died after a long and often painful illness and at the end seemed happy to go. Her children – four daughters – wept and mourned, and my friend in particular since she had been very close to her mother. After the undertaker had done his work, she was sitting weeping beside the coffin, bewailing the fact that she would never see her mother again, when she had a strong sense of her mother being near. She looked into the coffin and felt alienated by what she saw – her mother in a shroud not looking like herself. Calling her sisters, she got them to help her take their mother out of the coffin, take off the nasty nylon and redress her in a pretty housecoat. They put her own pillow back into the coffin and tucked in the soft blanket their mother had found such a comfort when she was ill. Into her hand my friend put her favourite small ornament and each of the sisters put something into the coffin that they thought she would like. The grandchildren were lifted up to see her and say goodbye and each added a small toy. Then the family stripped the roses from the garden and packed them round their mother in the coffin. As they were doing all this they were talking to her and to each other, sharing jokes and memories. The mourning was still real but it was combined with a joyful recognition that their mother's death was appropriate and timely. It has also changed my friend's perception of her own death. Although now only in her late forties, she has begun to think seriously about it.

What is as important as this story is its follow up. On describing what she and her sisters had done to friends and to professional colleagues the reaction uniformly was one of incredulity, followed by the question, 'But are you allowed to do that?' I find this very sad. Death and dying have been taken over by the professionals. I am not saying that there is no place for the professionals, but that place is in partnership with the person dying and with their family and friends. This is what the best professionals offer.

Kubler Ross shared Heidegger's view that one cannot fully live unless the inevitability of one's own demise is faced. Once death is unfearfully accepted, then one no longer fears to embrace the challenges constantly posed by life. Preparation for dying can be a new opening to life. Some of us have seen the liberating effects that a knowledge of approaching death can bring. Knowing we have nothing to lose can release us from all kinds of fears. The sadness for so many is that we have to wait until we know we're dying to liberate ourselves from the patterns imposed on us throughout our lives. Why wait? We can choose to die to something every day so that we can live to something new.

As we become older, giving up may become harder. We accumulate relationships and possessions that imprison us in habits and attitudes. We live in a time when ageing is deeply feared, when signs of ageing are attacked by the surgeon's knife, and so many regard their bodies as the enemy rather than as their best friend as it ought to be. The Bible talks about love driving out fear and we need to love our bodies if we are to die well in them. Those of us who keep open the possibility that some day we may choose the moment, the place and the style of our dying have to recognize the fact that, much though we might want it, our bodies will not simply evaporate. They will be left behind for someone to find and deal with. If we love our bodies and are comfortable with them we can make plans that will make that encounter as reasonable as it can possibly be. We can choose carefully what preparations we want to make. We might have an enema to avoid the bowels giving way. We will choose what we wear, the easiest form of death for us and the place in which we will be found. One friend of mine, a champion golfer, chose to die on a favourite golf course. The choice made sense to all of us who knew her and helped to make sense of her death. It is those who have lived their lives most fully who can let it go and prepare calmly to live their dying.

Living well means living each moment as it comes, neither bewailing the past nor fearing the future. It is not easy but whoever said that life was easy. This is the task that sages and mystics in all cultures have always set themselves. It is not as pompous as it sounds. The theologian Matthew Fox says his most important spiritual master is his dog. When they go for walks together the dog teaches him everything he needs to know about living in the moment as the dog explores with every sense the world in which he is moving. When we try to do this we become amazed at how short our attention span really is and how most of our life is spent in a sort of haze or blur. This consciousness can be applied to everything we do. If we are given a glass of wine or of medicine, instead of simply gulping it down as if it had nothing really to do with us we can turn that into an act of consciousness. This can give us an experience of wholeness, which can be healing both physically and spiritually. Most of all to live in the now we have to forgive ourselves for the mistakes and stupidities in which we have been involved. We have to respect that we did what we could with what we had at the time and let go of regrets.

I think I'm really talking about owning my life as of this moment, and in the same way I want to own my death. I do not want to see death as an enemy coming to me. I want to go to meet my death, not morbidly but in cooperation with the needs of my body and spirit. I may want to anticipate the actual moment at which my body if left to itself would yield up life. Or it may be that my body will make that decision in ways that are acceptable to me. I have a better chance of being able to recognize which of those things is happening if I have lived my dying throughout my life. As D.H.Lawrence said,

> 'O build your ship of death, O build it
> lovingly, and put it between the hands
> of your soul.'

Each of us needs to build our ship of death because for each of us our death will be unique. When the time comes, let us launch that ship with courage and a bit of style.

XII

THE END

The post-polio syndrome made Kay increasingly weak. It afflicts about half those who suffered severe paralysis in childhood as the muscles and nerves that were rebuilt to achieve some sort of recovery wear out. It was the muscles in her chest that were giving way. She would wake up in the night unable to breathe: a frightening experience. For some years she was able to keep this growing weakness under control with medication, but eventually that no longer worked. 'Don't worry Kay', said the consultant she mainly relied on, 'We have physical treatments that will keep you going.'

She returned from that consultation with her mind made up, facing an end we had often talked about. 'I'm not going down that road', she said. 'I would soon be in a nursing home breathing from an oxygen cylinder. You would come and visit me every day, wondering what on earth to say to me, and I would no longer be able to eat the grapes you brought.' Childhood memories of the nuns in the Order of St. Joseph of Cluny and the doctors in Glasgow's Royal Infirmary haunted her. She had already bought a shredder and destroyed papers she did not want to share with the world. The time had come to say goodbye to old friends and to her beloved grandchildren. Some recognized what was happening; some did not. This was a note she wrote at about this time.

...Have I lived? Somehow I have arrived here in my eighties – damaged in so many ways, having lost the experiences that made me feel I was living, they now just seem a dream as I wait, not anxiously, quite calmly – perhaps too calmly – for death. My questions are all about death and addressed to my death. Will you give me warning that you are near, working with me, letting me know when you become impatient to claim me? Will you allow me a peaceful, even dignified, end, giving me time to say goodbye? Perhaps you will come quietly in the night allowing me a last deep gasp of air? I know you can't tell me, but I'm curious and would like to know.

...Ceasing to believe in hell or heaven came as a great relief. I could see death as a friend... no longer as something to fear...

She acquired a drug used by the Swiss enterprises that help people to end their lives, and bought a new and attractive night dress, ironing it carefully for the day when it would be needed. Her daughter and son-in-law joined us for Christmas in 2006 and we had a great meal together. Next day she wrote and signed a letter. This is it – the last document in this collection.

December 26th, 2009

As my time comes to leave this world I want to say that I have had an interesting and happy life which has continued for longer than I had any right to expect, but I am now experiencing increasing pain and helplessness which can only grow worse. Thus, while I am still mentally and physically capable of making this decision and carrying it out, I am bringing my life to an end.

I am grateful to the many doctors and nurses of the N.H.S. who have helped me to get this far and who frankly explained what lies ahead, and to my loved ones who will be accompanying me through these final hours. None of them have encouraged or assisted me in this act, which is entirely my own responsibility.

When the time came for her afternoon nap Kay said goodbye to us, took to her bed and drank the draught she had prepared. I sat beside her holding her hand. With grace and gallantry, looking beautiful, she ceased breathing in four minutes.

Recalling the stories told by those who have had near-death out-of -body experiences – experiences she had had in her youth – I wondered if she was looking down at us from the ceiling. I looked up and said 'Goodbye my darling. I love you... Safe journey.'

XIII

ANSWERS TO KAY'S QUESTION

I began this collection of Kay's writings with my recollection of the remark she made in 1975 about the book she never wrote. It would have asked: Why is it that some children, who grow up handicapped in many ways, without consistent and reliable affection, bearing all the marks of a doom-laden future, nevertheless do quite well and make a significant contribution to the world? It was much later that I realised it was her own story she was reflecting on. It would have made a useful case study in such a book. There are many parts of her story I know nothing about, but the writings gathered here tell enough about her life to make us wonder what conclusions her own experience might have contributed to her unwritten book.

My readers will have their own answers to her question. These are mine.

Kay was clearly an able child who became an able woman, learning to read widely and fast at an early age and greatly enjoying doing so, educating herself in the public library when abandoned by the education system for four formative years, awarded the title of 'Dux' – top scholar – in the Glasgow secondary school to which she returned at the age of seventeen. Kay was then accepted by Glasgow University's medical school (once, and then again before her intermittent education twice failed her), recruited later to the University's staff, promoted, and soon invited to do other demanding jobs. The evidence is clear. 'I never applied for a job', she once told me. 'People just asked me to come and help them.'

She was also independent and courageous: successfully defying the appalling tyranny of the nuns at the age of four and five; making her escape at thirteen from an intolerable home life by getting herself evacuated to rural Dumfriesshire and finding her feet there in four households of different kinds – the chicken farm, the pig farm, the Manse, and Mrs Dickson's dower house. Throughout her life she was dogged by the pain and hardship inflicted by polio, which undoubtedly left her somewhat brain-damaged (her own description). Yet she bore and raised an able daughter and helped to manage her husband's constituency while making her mark in the intellectual and political worlds of Glasgow, Scotland and London, without any social advantages other than those she created for herself – and eventually going to prison for her pacifist principals where she defied authority again with wit and style. Her scholarly but practical interest in moral philosophy and literature stayed with her to the end as any reader of her book, 'Sin and Forgiveness', completed and published when she was 77, will recognise.

I make these points not because Kay needs a eulogy, but to remind us that few normal children surmount such difficult early years unscathed. This was a very unusual child who became an unusually talented woman. Many other youngsters' lives have been ruined by the kind of experiences she went through – as she well knew, having worked with them as a social worker and in Barlinnie's Special Unit, which housed some of Scotland's most violent men.

What else explains her survival and success? People, mainly. Most important was her grandmother, whom she described as the 'peasant-like woman' who 'saved her sanity' and was 'always there for her'' – until her mother took her away at the age of four and sent her to the nuns. There she found Mother Theresa, 'an aged and crumpled little woman' who taught her to read. 'She knew what she was giving me and somewhere our souls met. It was to be my only good experience in the convent.'

Later, as an evacuee, between the ages of thirteen and seventeen, she learnt new ways of living – new social possibilities – most importantly from Mrs. Dickson – the widow she stayed with who knew everyone from the Royal Family downward. She described Mrs. Dickson as teaching her much more about economics and the British class system than the Marxist classics she was already reading. Local farm workers, who welcomed this young teenager to the shop – their informal club – where they recited radical poetry by Robert Burns and others, played an important part in her life too. Back in Glasgow at the age of seventeen, she joined the Independent Labour Party, which gave her what she described as the most valuable higher education she received. There were many other influences she discovered for herself: Marx and Freud, novels, films and literature of many kinds which later helped her to make an important contribution to a weekly Radio Scotland programme on the creative arts, and eventually to write her own book on Sin and Forgiveness with its massive bibliography. The people, the books, plays and films did not enter her life by accident. She sought them out for herself, making frequent use of public libraries for the purpose.

What other factors played a part in Kay's story? Travel was somewhere in the mix. She loved visiting other countries and, before she was through, Mexico, China, Burma, Ireland, Paris, New York and California were among the places that fascinated and delighted her. Her visit to Japan and the week it enabled her to spend in a Buddhist monastery changed her life. Yet she always knew that Scotland – and Glasgow in particular – was her home. Although she was offered important jobs in London, she turned down any that would have compelled her to move her main home from the West of Scotland. That was where she was rooted, among her many friends.

If these glimpses of her story suggest it was an effortless progress to success, that would be entirely mistaken. Kay was constantly reflecting on her own life and the moral values that guided her, and at times suffered deep grief and bouts of depression. It was then particularly that she drew on her capacity for finding and using the help of 'shamans', as she sometimes called them – a capacity first learnt as a child from Michael Cooney, the crippled Irish masseur who lived along the street from her home in the East End of Glasgow. Some of these men – and they were mostly men – were professionally qualified therapists; others, like Cooney, were largely self-taught. She knew how to recognise them and use their help, and often they learned as much from her.

She was a natural healer. Men and women of all ages and social classes found they made lifelong friendships with her. Former social work clients and constituents – and their children – were still in touch with her till her last years. Two of the many moving tributes written for her funeral may serve to illustrate this.

> '...an extraordinary powerful spiritual mischievous dedicated, and above all human being ...a naughty dignified compassionate rebel with a cause... Kay lives until there is no one left to remember... this wonderful woman.'
>
> – Anthony (Lord) Lester.

> 'Some people would have been afraid or not cared.
> Not even answered the door at that unearthly hour.
> But Kay Carmichael did'.
>
> – Ruth Dunster.

Kay kept alive her capacity for protest till the end of her life – the capacity that ultimately shaped the manner of her death. This rebellious instinct was what enabled her to confront and survive Mother Stanislaus and to work so successfully with Borstal boys and girls and the violent men who were sent to the Special Unit in Barlinnie prison. Deep down, she had an affinity with them, knowing that she could have been one of them. When required to name her profession she often described herself as an 'activist'. In the business of government she was an instinctive critic and 'oppositionist'. It was this, I believe, that eventually broke up her marriage with that well-loved Labour politician, Neil Carmichael, whose instinct was to play the opposite and equally needed political role as one of Plato's 'guardians'.

XIV

REQUIEM

I offer some of my own poems, published two years after Kay's death by Playspace Publications, as a postscript to her book.

Many of us have at some point in our lives to pass through a loss so catastrophic that we have to create for ourselves a new life – a new identity. When Kay died I felt a need to put down words to help me find a way through a vale of tears. I instinctively resorted to poetic forms to convey the pain and passion and to seek the sharper edge to thought that poetry makes possible. The pages that follow can be read as one poem: first some premonitions, then a journal of grief, presented roughly in the order in which it was written. I have added at the foot of each poem the date at which it took something like its final shape.

VALENTINE

When we first met 'fey' was the word that came to mind;
not sure what it meant – but it spoke to me.
'Strange, clairvoyant, elfin, other-worldly' says my
O.E.D.
Thirty-six years on, no better word can I find.

14.2.08

DANGEROUS COMMITMENT

For thirty years I have hesitantly learnt
to risk commitment – passionate, total –
to this astonishing woman,
knowing well that on some distant day
a small boy must pack his bag again,
set off once more in the bleak and bitter rain.

15.1.10

AS DEATH IMPENDS

As death impends self-centred I become,
battening down the hatches
as the roar of loss approaches.

Grief seeps deep through my bones;
the busy crowd irrelevant –
citizens of a distant, half-heard world.

Time disintegrates. This tea and toast,
so carefully carried, fills all eternity.
Next week? Next month....? Who cares?

30.11.09

ALONE

And now....?

Small things remain the same:
wash the dishes, fold the clothes,
tend the murmuring stove.
Trivially busy, I rove about;
homeless in my home;
haunted at every step.
The door code? Her birthday date.
Pictures ? Sculptures?
I remember where we bought each one,
Why she liked them, what she said...

Her slippers peep from under the bed.

30.1.10

SURVIVING

Life will never be the same
so – different I shall make it;
new places, faces...
I shall survive, appear to thrive;
surfing the cheerful chatter
of this ever-turning world,

10.2.10

SCATTERING YOUR ASHES

I come to this rock
where you would sit
to say goodbye
to your life and mine.

I come to pray –
not for you but to you –
seeking a share
in your lonely gallantry.

Gazing here together
to the Atlantic horizon,
'There is no path' you said.
'We make the path by walking'.

Now I must walk,
travelling light,
till our dust mingles
in these flowing tides.

Rolling slowly homewards
I drive sedately.
No need for speed.
No one to get home to.

22.2.10

LONELY ON THE SHORE

'So where did you scatter her ashes?' he asked,
and I told him of that wave-washed rock.
'Many' he said, 'have ended there'.

You'd be content, I felt
to mingle with neighbours
in that rolling sea.

As for me – my aching pain
is no more than the price all pay
for love left lonely on the shore.

10.3.10

A MESSAGE

'You are looking
at the person responsible
for your health and happiness' –
words she inscribed
on the bathroom mirror.

They spoke to me
like a shaft through the heart.

15.5.10

MOVING HOUSE

This house that framed our lives
disintegrates around me,
books and papers, chairs and tables,
spoken for by family,
heading for dealers and charity shops –
all borne away.

I recall where we found them,
why you loved them, what we said.
Markers trace your footsteps through pages of your books,
leave questions in the air.
Now the talk is done
- nothing more to say.

Things outlive their owners; play new parts in other lives.
To each we give brief meaning
before we let them go to folk who'll never know
the joys and pains they brought us.
Naked at our birth, we'll be naked once again
at the ending of the day.

11.5.10

JOURNEYING ONWARDS

Taking the road through this lovely country
to which you brought me half a lifetime ago,
you drive at my side every mile of the way
as I recall scenes we saw,
places we paused, things you said ….
and I pray to you, comrade and lover,
for comfort, a compass, on life's rocky road,
nailing these thoughts in my aching brain. How lucky I've
been! Say it again.
Lucky I've been…For thirty long years.
Now the pain is no longer yours.
For all must die, but few so frail
survive so long. I too survived:
to care, to share your final triumph,
gallant and graceful, holding my hand
to the very end ….

Thoughts I cling to – a raft in the darkness,
nailed frailly together.

27.4.10

TIME PASSING

On the road to Morley's Bridge, County Kerry.

Thirty years back we paused by this torrent
carving its chasm through bronzed rocks.

My picture shows you in pride and prime –
triumphant, windswept, wild.

Twenty years later, passing again,
my picture shows you older but elegant.

Today I stand before an empty space –
appalling roar of falling waters.

High in the sky turbines now turn.
Their whirling blades, far and faint,
make a rhythmic cry, driven by winds
and bearing ashes of the multitudinous dead.

29.5.10

GODLESS PRAYER

With no predestined fate,
neither tragic nor triumphant,
we must take each day that's sent us –
create it and shape it.

Hunters and gatherers
from time immemorial,
we make our paths by walking –
write each our own story.

So turn grieving to gratitude,
knowing each bitter dawn
offers scope for hope –
liberty of the lonely.

23.7.10

MOVING ON

Slowly, slowly you are leaving me –
your living, breathing presence
woven through each thing I do,
distancing me from the passing throng.

Now each day I seek
a quiet and private space
to talk with you, stilling
my spirit in a kind of prayer.

Our shared lives drift into history –
blissful history,
but gone for ever –
as I return to the busy world,
the sea in which I sink or swim.

24.8.10

AN INJURY

Pain has many guises –
the stalker threatening my day,
assailant gnawing at my flesh,
heart-sink friend who never goes away.

I long for the healing hand
that you would gently lay
upon my wincing skin –
taking all my pain away

6.10.10

FROM BEYOND THE GRAVE

Catastrophic loss, you said,
impales us like barbed wire.
Turn your back upon it – pull away –
its teeth will rend your soul.

Embrace the pain and face it,
then gently disentangle –
grateful for memories
that will some day make you whole.

13.11.10

GRIEVING FOR THE WORLD

Rationalising grief
I've got my act together,
raised my game.

Not exactly cheerful
but purposeful, not tearful,
planning a future –

till my foot breaks through
thin ice of reason
into caverns of pain.

Then tears flow again,
not just for you,
my lost and only lover.

Every life ends in tragedy –
each a brief spark of gallantry
defying darkness to come.

24.11.10

ANOTHER FROZEN CHRISTMAS

Listening alone to carols I hear
of gold and frankincense and myrrh –
symbols of the season.

What symbols speak for you and me
on this your anniversary –
devotee of reason?

For you perhaps the blazing beauty
of the frost. For me the call to duty
of the returning sun.

26.12.10 (Anniversary of her death)

LONELY PEAK EXPERIENCE

Darkness falls on the turning world.
Soon the Plough and far Orion
set the night alight.

I contemplate the scale of things –
puny irrelevance of the human race,
terror of space…

It's then I need a comrade to hear my orisons,
to respond, to bond; bring me gently home
from infinite horizons.

12.1.11

LOCH GARTEN SHORE

Sun slants brilliant through pines,
their roots writhing in a pathway of needles
that winds for miles along this shore.

I recall past years, walking with you
deep in these woods; then in recent times
at a gentler pace, your hand in mine;

till came the day when I did the walking.
You sat in the car, gazed down the loch.
Now I walk alone; will follow you soon.

But this path will wind, the sun still shine,
and scent of the pines still wreathe among wraithes
of all whose love sanctifies this place.

17.5.11

AT THE END OF THE DAY

What matters most at the end of the day?
To have been loved with passion, total commitment,
demanding only the same of me.
Not floating gently down the stream
but a wild voyage through sun and storm –
rainbows dancing all the way.

All things change, come to an end.
Though wrecked in grief, I've been so blessed
I know for sure I can survive
And – come the day – will die content.

21.6.11

LAST POST

We are an army, marching under fire;
no victory ahead; unable to retire.
Every year my comrades fall,
far and near I hear them call.

Debonair, philandering Sandy
teeters on a frame, too frail to be randy.
Peter, gently witty, gave us laughter all his life;
don't see him now; he's caring for his wife.
Tony, mountaineer – intelligence unrelenting –
only shuffles; quietly dementing.
Journalist Joe – fastest pen in the west –
waits patiently in hospitals for another test.
Jehu John rides a howling Honda;
will take off on high – go burning up the sky.

We are an army advancing to our doom.
Time is done for dancing; can't body-swerve the tomb.
So come, my tottering comrades, defy the passing bell;
courageous, outrageous – we'll storm the gates of Hell!

7.1.09

POSTSCRIPT

Thought you wrote some poems?
You were wrong.
Powered by pain,
half scream, half song,
they kept your head to wind,
drove you through the storm.
The poems wrote you.

19.6.10

Acknowledgements

Many people have given me practical help and personal encouragement as I was putting this collection of Kay's writings together.

I'm grateful to all of them, and particularly wish to thank Larry Butler, Sheena Carmichael, Roz Ryan-Mills, Bev Schofield, Cathie Thomson, and the archivists of Glasgow University.

D.D.